FREE Study Skills Videos/DVD Offer

Dear Customer,

Thank you for your purchase from Mometrix! We consider it an honor and a privilege that you have purchased our product and we want to ensure your satisfaction.

As part of our ongoing effort to meet the needs of test takers, we have developed a set of Study Skills Videos that we would like to give you for <u>FREE</u>. These videos cover our *best practices* for getting ready for your exam, from how to use our study materials to how to best prepare for the day of the test.

All that we ask is that you email us with feedback that would describe your experience so far with our product. Good, bad, or indifferent, we want to know what you think!

To get your FREE Study Skills Videos, you can use the **QR code** below, or send us an **email** at studyvideos@mometrix.com with *FREE VIDEOS* in the subject line and the following information in the body of the email:

- The name of the product you purchased.
- Your product rating on a scale of 1-5, with 5 being the highest rating.
- Your feedback. It can be long, short, or anything in between. We just want to know your impressions and experience so far with our product. (Good feedback might include how our study material met your needs and ways we might be able to make it even better. You could highlight features that you found helpful or features that you think we should add.)

If you have any questions or concerns, please don't hesitate to contact me directly.

Thanks again!

Sincerely,

Jay Willis
Vice President
jay.willis@mometrix.com
1-800-673-8175

SCAN HERE

SIE

Exam Prep 2023 and 2024

3 Full-Length Practice Tests

Secrets Study Guide Book for the FINRA Securities Industry Essentials

4th Edition

Written and edited by the Mometrix Financial Industry Certification Test Team

Printed in the United States of America

This paper meets the requirements of ANSI/NISO Z39.48-1992 (Permanence of Paper).

Mometrix offers volume discount pricing to institutions. For more information or a price quote, please contact our sales department at sales@mometrix.com or 888-248-1219.

Mometrix Media LLC is not affiliated with or endorsed by any official testing organization. All organizational and test names are trademarks of their respective owners.

ISBN 13: 978-1-5167-2285-3
ISBN 10: 1-5167-2285-X

Dear Future Exam Success Story

First of all, **THANK YOU** for purchasing Mometrix study materials!

Second, congratulations! You are one of the few determined test-takers who are committed to doing whatever it takes to excel on your exam. **You have come to the right place.** We developed these study materials with one goal in mind: to deliver you the information you need in a format that's concise and easy to use.

In addition to optimizing your guide for the content of the test, we've outlined our recommended steps for breaking down the preparation process into small, attainable goals so you can make sure you stay on track.

We've also analyzed the entire test-taking process, identifying the most common pitfalls and showing how you can overcome them and be ready for any curveball the test throws you.

Standardized testing is one of the biggest obstacles on your road to success, which only increases the importance of doing well in the high-pressure, high-stakes environment of test day. Your results on this test could have a significant impact on your future, and this guide provides the information and practical advice to help you achieve your full potential on test day.

Your success is our success

We would love to hear from you! If you would like to share the story of your exam success or if you have any questions or comments in regard to our products, please contact us at **800-673-8175** or **support@mometrix.com**.

Thanks again for your business and we wish you continued success!

Sincerely,
The Mometrix Test Preparation Team

Need more help? Check out our flashcards at:
http://mometrixflashcards.com/SeriesSIE

TABLE OF CONTENTS

Introduction

Thank you for purchasing this resource! You have made the choice to prepare yourself for a test that could have a huge impact on your future, and this guide is designed to help you be fully ready for test day. Obviously, it's important to have a solid understanding of the test material, but you also need to be prepared for the unique environment and stressors of the test, so that you can perform to the best of your abilities.

For this purpose, the first section that appears in this guide is the **Secret Keys**. We've devoted countless hours to meticulously researching what works and what doesn't, and we've boiled down our findings to the five most impactful steps you can take to improve your performance on the test. We start at the beginning with study planning and move through the preparation process, all the way to the testing strategies that will help you get the most out of what you know when you're finally sitting in front of the test.

We recommend that you start preparing for your test as far in advance as possible. However, if you've bought this guide as a last-minute study resource and only have a few days before your test, we recommend that you skip over the first two Secret Keys since they address a long-term study plan.

If you struggle with **test anxiety**, we strongly encourage you to check out our recommendations for how you can overcome it. Test anxiety is a formidable foe, but it can be beaten, and we want to make sure you have the tools you need to defeat it.

Secret Key #1 – Plan Big, Study Small

There's a lot riding on your performance. If you want to ace this test, you're going to need to keep your skills sharp and the material fresh in your mind. You need a plan that lets you review everything you need to know while still fitting in your schedule. We'll break this strategy down into three categories.

Information Organization

Start with the information you already have: the official test outline. From this, you can make a complete list of all the concepts you need to cover before the test. Organize these concepts into groups that can be studied together, and create a list of any related vocabulary you need to learn so you can brush up on any difficult terms. You'll want to keep this vocabulary list handy once you actually start studying since you may need to add to it along the way.

Time Management

Once you have your set of study concepts, decide how to spread them out over the time you have left before the test. Break your study plan into small, clear goals so you have a manageable task for each day and know exactly what you're doing. Then just focus on one small step at a time. When you manage your time this way, you don't need to spend hours at a time studying. Studying a small block of content for a short period each day helps you retain information better and avoid stressing over how much you have left to do. You can relax knowing that you have a plan to cover everything in time. In order for this strategy to be effective though, you have to start studying early and stick to your schedule. Avoid the exhaustion and futility that comes from last-minute cramming!

Study Environment

The environment you study in has a big impact on your learning. Studying in a coffee shop, while probably more enjoyable, is not likely to be as fruitful as studying in a quiet room. It's important to keep distractions to a minimum. You're only planning to study for a short block of time, so make the most of it. Don't pause to check your phone or get up to find a snack. It's also important to **avoid multitasking**. Research has consistently shown that multitasking will make your studying dramatically less effective. Your study area should also be comfortable and well-lit so you don't have the distraction of straining your eyes or sitting on an uncomfortable chair.

 The time of day you study is also important. You want to be rested and alert. Don't wait until just before bedtime. Study when you'll be most likely to comprehend and remember. Even better, if you know what time of day your test will be, set that time aside for study. That way your brain will be used to working on that subject at that specific time and you'll have a better chance of recalling information.

Finally, it can be helpful to team up with others who are studying for the same test. Your actual studying should be done in as isolated an environment as possible, but the work of organizing the information and setting up the study plan can be divided up. In between study sessions, you can discuss with your teammates the concepts that you're all studying and quiz each other on the details. Just be sure that your teammates are as serious about the test as you are. If you find that your study time is being replaced with social time, you might need to find a new team.

Secret Key #2 – Make Your Studying Count

You're devoting a lot of time and effort to preparing for this test, so you want to be absolutely certain it will pay off. This means doing more than just reading the content and hoping you can remember it on test day. It's important to make every minute of study count. There are two main areas you can focus on to make your studying count.

Retention

It doesn't matter how much time you study if you can't remember the material. You need to make sure you are retaining the concepts. To check your retention of the information you're learning, try recalling it at later times with minimal prompting. Try carrying around flashcards and glance at one or two from time to time or ask a friend who's also studying for the test to quiz you.

To enhance your retention, look for ways to put the information into practice so that you can apply it rather than simply recalling it. If you're using the information in practical ways, it will be much easier to remember. Similarly, it helps to solidify a concept in your mind if you're not only reading it to yourself but also explaining it to someone else. Ask a friend to let you teach them about a concept you're a little shaky on (or speak aloud to an imaginary audience if necessary). As you try to summarize, define, give examples, and answer your friend's questions, you'll understand the concepts better and they will stay with you longer. Finally, step back for a big picture view and ask yourself how each piece of information fits with the whole subject. When you link the different concepts together and see them working together as a whole, it's easier to remember the individual components.

Finally, practice showing your work on any multi-step problems, even if you're just studying. Writing out each step you take to solve a problem will help solidify the process in your mind, and you'll be more likely to remember it during the test.

Modality

Modality simply refers to the means or method by which you study. Choosing a study modality that fits your own individual learning style is crucial. No two people learn best in exactly the same way, so it's important to know your strengths and use them to your advantage.

For example, if you learn best by visualization, focus on visualizing a concept in your mind and draw an image or a diagram. Try color-coding your notes, illustrating them, or creating symbols that will trigger your mind to recall a learned concept. If you learn best by hearing or discussing information, find a study partner who learns the same way or read aloud to yourself. Think about how to put the information in your own words. Imagine that you are giving a lecture on the topic and record yourself so you can listen to it later.

For any learning style, flashcards can be helpful. Organize the information so you can take advantage of spare moments to review. Underline key words or phrases. Use different colors for different categories. Mnemonic devices (such as creating a short list in which every item starts with the same letter) can also help with retention. Find what works best for you and use it to store the information in your mind most effectively and easily.

Secret Key #3 – Practice the Right Way

Your success on test day depends not only on how many hours you put into preparing, but also on whether you prepared the right way. It's good to check along the way to see if your studying is paying off. One of the most effective ways to do this is by taking practice tests to evaluate your progress. Practice tests are useful because they show exactly where you need to improve. Every time you take a practice test, pay special attention to these three groups of questions:

- The questions you got wrong
- The questions you had to guess on, even if you guessed right
- The questions you found difficult or slow to work through

This will show you exactly what your weak areas are, and where you need to devote more study time. Ask yourself why each of these questions gave you trouble. Was it because you didn't understand the material? Was it because you didn't remember the vocabulary? Do you need more repetitions on this type of question to build speed and confidence? Dig into those questions and figure out how you can strengthen your weak areas as you go back to review the material.

 Additionally, many practice tests have a section explaining the answer choices. It can be tempting to read the explanation and think that you now have a good understanding of the concept. However, an explanation likely only covers part of the question's broader context. Even if the explanation makes perfect sense, **go back and investigate** every concept related to the question until you're positive you have a thorough understanding.

As you go along, keep in mind that the practice test is just that: practice. Memorizing these questions and answers will not be very helpful on the actual test because it is unlikely to have any of the same exact questions. If you only know the right answers to the sample questions, you won't be prepared for the real thing. **Study the concepts** until you understand them fully, and then you'll be able to answer any question that shows up on the test.

It's important to wait on the practice tests until you're ready. If you take a test on your first day of study, you may be overwhelmed by the amount of material covered and how much you need to learn. Work up to it gradually.

On test day, you'll need to be prepared for answering questions, managing your time, and using the test-taking strategies you've learned. It's a lot to balance, like a mental marathon that will have a big impact on your future. Like training for a marathon, you'll need to start slowly and work your way up. When test day arrives, you'll be ready.

Start with the strategies you've read in the first two Secret Keys—plan your course and study in the way that works best for you. If you have time, consider using multiple study resources to get different approaches to the same concepts. It can be helpful to see difficult concepts from more than one angle. Then find a good source for practice tests. Many times, the test website will suggest potential study resources or provide sample tests.

4

Practice Test Strategy

If you're able to find at least three practice tests, we recommend this strategy:

UNTIMED AND OPEN-BOOK PRACTICE

Take the first test with no time constraints and with your notes and study guide handy. Take your time and focus on applying the strategies you've learned.

TIMED AND OPEN-BOOK PRACTICE

Take the second practice test open-book as well, but set a timer and practice pacing yourself to finish in time.

TIMED AND CLOSED-BOOK PRACTICE

Take any other practice tests as if it were test day. Set a timer and put away your study materials. Sit at a table or desk in a quiet room, imagine yourself at the testing center, and answer questions as quickly and accurately as possible.

Keep repeating timed and closed-book tests on a regular basis until you run out of practice tests or it's time for the actual test. Your mind will be ready for the schedule and stress of test day, and you'll be able to focus on recalling the material you've learned.

Secret Key #4 – Pace Yourself

Once you're fully prepared for the material on the test, your biggest challenge on test day will be managing your time. Just knowing that the clock is ticking can make you panic even if you have plenty of time left. Work on pacing yourself so you can build confidence against the time constraints of the exam. Pacing is a difficult skill to master, especially in a high-pressure environment, so **practice is vital**.

Set time expectations for your pace based on how much time is available. For example, if a section has 60 questions and the time limit is 30 minutes, you know you have to average 30 seconds or less per question in order to answer them all. Although 30 seconds is the hard limit, set 25 seconds per question as your goal, so you reserve extra time to spend on harder questions. When you budget extra time for the harder questions, you no longer have any reason to stress when those questions take longer to answer.

Don't let this time expectation distract you from working through the test at a calm, steady pace, but keep it in mind so you don't spend too much time on any one question. Recognize that taking extra time on one question you don't understand may keep you from answering two that you do understand later in the test. If your time limit for a question is up and you're still not sure of the answer, mark it and move on, and come back to it later if the time and the test format allow. If the testing format doesn't allow you to return to earlier questions, just make an educated guess; then put it out of your mind and move on.

On the easier questions, be careful not to rush. It may seem wise to hurry through them so you have more time for the challenging ones, but it's not worth missing one if you know the concept and just didn't take the time to read the question fully. Work efficiently but make sure you understand the question and have looked at all of the answer choices, since more than one may seem right at first.

Even if you're paying attention to the time, you may find yourself a little behind at some point. You should speed up to get back on track, but do so wisely. Don't panic; just take a few seconds less on each question until you're caught up. Don't guess without thinking, but do look through the answer choices and eliminate any you know are wrong. If you can get down to two choices, it is often worthwhile to guess from those. Once you've chosen an answer, move on and don't dwell on any that you skipped or had to hurry through. If a question was taking too long, chances are it was one of the harder ones, so you weren't as likely to get it right anyway.

On the other hand, if you find yourself getting ahead of schedule, it may be beneficial to slow down a little. The more quickly you work, the more likely you are to make a careless mistake that will affect your score. You've budgeted time for each question, so don't be afraid to spend that time. Practice an efficient but careful pace to get the most out of the time you have.

6

Secret Key #5 – Have a Plan for Guessing

When you're taking the test, you may find yourself stuck on a question. Some of the answer choices seem better than others, but you don't see the one answer choice that is obviously correct. What do you do?

The scenario described above is very common, yet most test takers have not effectively prepared for it. Developing and practicing a plan for guessing may be one of the single most effective uses of your time as you get ready for the exam.

In developing your plan for guessing, there are three questions to address:

- When should you start the guessing process?
- How should you narrow down the choices?
- Which answer should you choose?

When to Start the Guessing Process

Unless your plan for guessing is to select C every time (which, despite its merits, is not what we recommend), you need to leave yourself enough time to apply your answer elimination strategies. Since you have a limited amount of time for each question, that means that if you're going to give yourself the best shot at guessing correctly, you have to decide quickly whether or not you will guess.

Of course, the best-case scenario is that you don't have to guess at all, so first, see if you can answer the question based on your knowledge of the subject and basic reasoning skills. Focus on the key words in the question and try to jog your memory of related topics. Give yourself a chance to bring the knowledge to mind, but once you realize that you don't have (or you can't access) the knowledge you need to answer the question, it's time to start the guessing process.

It's almost always better to start the guessing process too early than too late. It only takes a few seconds to remember something and answer the question from knowledge. Carefully eliminating wrong answer choices takes longer. Plus, going through the process of eliminating answer choices can actually help jog your memory.

Summary: Start the guessing process as soon as you decide that you can't answer the question based on your knowledge.

7

How to Narrow Down the Choices

The next chapter in this book (**Test-Taking Strategies**) includes a wide range of strategies for how to approach questions and how to look for answer choices to eliminate. You will definitely want to read those carefully, practice them, and figure out which ones work best for you. Here though, we're going to address a mindset rather than a particular strategy.

Your odds of guessing an answer correctly depend on how many options you are choosing from.

Number of options left	5	4	3	2	1
Odds of guessing correctly	20%	25%	33%	50%	100%

You can see from this chart just how valuable it is to be able to eliminate incorrect answers and make an educated guess, but there are two things that many test takers do that cause them to miss out on the benefits of guessing:

- Accidentally eliminating the correct answer
- Selecting an answer based on an impression

We'll look at the first one here, and the second one in the next section.

To avoid accidentally eliminating the correct answer, we recommend a thought exercise called **the $5 challenge**. In this challenge, you only eliminate an answer choice from contention if you are willing to bet $5 on it being wrong. Why $5? Five dollars is a small but not insignificant amount of money. It's an amount you could afford to lose but wouldn't want to throw away. And while losing

$5 once might not hurt too much, doing it twenty times will set you back $100. In the same way, each small decision you make—eliminating a choice here, guessing on a question there—won't by itself impact your score very much, but when you put them all together, they can make a big difference. By holding each answer choice elimination decision to a higher standard, you can reduce the risk of accidentally eliminating the correct answer.

The $5 challenge can also be applied in a positive sense: If you are willing to bet $5 that an answer choice *is* correct, go ahead and mark it as correct.

Summary: Only eliminate an answer choice if you are willing to bet $5 that it is wrong.

8

Which Answer to Choose

You're taking the test. You've run into a hard question and decided you'll have to guess. You've eliminated all the answer choices you're willing to bet $5 on. Now you have to pick an answer. Why do we even need to talk about this? Why can't you just pick whichever one you feel like when the time comes?

The answer to these questions is that if you don't come into the test with a plan, you'll rely on your impression to select an answer choice, and if you do that, you risk falling into a trap. The test writers know that everyone who takes their test will be guessing on some of the questions, so they intentionally write wrong answer choices to seem plausible. You still have to pick an answer though, and if the wrong answer choices are designed to look right, how can you ever be sure that you're not falling for their trap? The best solution we've found to this dilemma is to take the decision out of your hands entirely. Here is the process we recommend:

Once you've eliminated any choices that you are confident (willing to bet $5) are wrong, select the first remaining choice as your answer.

Whether you choose to select the first remaining choice, the second, or the last, the important thing is that you use some preselected standard. Using this approach guarantees that you will not be enticed into selecting an answer choice that looks right, because you are not basing your decision on how the answer choices look.

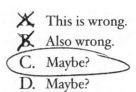

This is not meant to make you question your knowledge. Instead, it is to help you recognize the difference between your knowledge and your impressions. There's a huge difference between thinking an answer is right because of what you know, and thinking an answer is right because it looks or sounds like it should be right.

Summary: To ensure that your selection is appropriately random, make a predetermined selection from among all answer choices you have not eliminated.

Test-Taking Strategies

This section contains a list of test-taking strategies that you may find helpful as you work through the test. By taking what you know and applying logical thought, you can maximize your chances of answering any question correctly!

It is very important to realize that every question is different and every person is different: no single strategy will work on every question, and no single strategy will work for every person. That's why we've included all of them here, so you can try them out and determine which ones work best for different types of questions and which ones work best for you.

Question Strategies

⦿ READ CAREFULLY

Read the question and the answer choices carefully. Don't miss the question because you misread the terms. You have plenty of time to read each question thoroughly and make sure you understand what is being asked. Yet a happy medium must be attained, so don't waste too much time. You must read carefully and efficiently.

⦿ CONTEXTUAL CLUES

Look for contextual clues. If the question includes a word you are not familiar with, look at the immediate context for some indication of what the word might mean. Contextual clues can often give you all the information you need to decipher the meaning of an unfamiliar word. Even if you can't determine the meaning, you may be able to narrow down the possibilities enough to make a solid guess at the answer to the question.

⦿ PREFIXES

If you're having trouble with a word in the question or answer choices, try dissecting it. Take advantage of every clue that the word might include. Prefixes can be a huge help. Usually, they allow you to determine a basic meaning. *Pre-* means before, *post-* means after, *pro-* is positive, *de-* is negative. From prefixes, you can get an idea of the general meaning of the word and try to put it into context.

⦿ HEDGE WORDS

Watch out for critical hedge words, such as *likely, may, can, sometimes, often, almost, mostly, usually, generally, rarely,* and *sometimes.* Question writers insert these hedge phrases to cover every possibility. Often an answer choice will be wrong simply because it leaves no room for exception. Be on guard for answer choices that have definitive words such as *exactly* and *always.*

⦿ SWITCHBACK WORDS

Stay alert for *switchbacks*. These are the words and phrases frequently used to alert you to shifts in thought. The most common switchback words are *but, although,* and *however.* Others include *nevertheless, on the other hand, even though, while, in spite of, despite,* and *regardless of.* Switchback words are important to catch because they can change the direction of the question or an answer choice.

10

⊘ FACE VALUE

When in doubt, use common sense. Accept the situation in the problem at face value. Don't read too much into it. These problems will not require you to make wild assumptions. If you have to go beyond creativity and warp time or space in order to have an answer choice fit the question, then you should move on and consider the other answer choices. These are normal problems rooted in reality. The applicable relationship or explanation may not be readily apparent, but it is there for you to figure out. Use your common sense to interpret anything that isn't clear.

Answer Choice Strategies

⊘ ANSWER SELECTION

The most thorough way to pick an answer choice is to identify and eliminate wrong answers until only one is left, then confirm it is the correct answer. Sometimes an answer choice may immediately seem right, but be careful. The test writers will usually put more than one reasonable answer choice on each question, so take a second to read all of them and make sure that the other choices are not equally obvious. As long as you have time left, it is better to read every answer choice than to pick the first one that looks right without checking the others.

⊘ ANSWER CHOICE FAMILIES

An answer choice family consists of two (in rare cases, three) answer choices that are very similar in construction and cannot all be true at the same time. If you see two answer choices that are direct opposites or parallels, one of them is usually the correct answer. For instance, if one answer choice says that quantity x increases and another either says that quantity x decreases (opposite) or says that quantity y increases (parallel), then those answer choices would fall into the same family. An answer choice that doesn't match the construction of the answer choice family is more likely to be incorrect. Most questions will not have answer choice families, but when they do appear, you should be prepared to recognize them.

⊘ ELIMINATE ANSWERS

Eliminate answer choices as soon as you realize they are wrong, but make sure you consider all possibilities. If you are eliminating answer choices and realize that the last one you are left with is also wrong, don't panic. Start over and consider each choice again. There may be something you missed the first time that you will realize on the second pass.

⊘ AVOID FACT TRAPS

Don't be distracted by an answer choice that is factually true but doesn't answer the question. You are looking for the choice that answers the question. Stay focused on what the question is asking for so you don't accidentally pick an answer that is true but incorrect. Always go back to the question and make sure the answer choice you've selected actually answers the question and is not merely a true statement.

⊘ EXTREME STATEMENTS

In general, you should avoid answers that put forth extreme actions as standard practice or proclaim controversial ideas as established fact. An answer choice that states the "process should be used in certain situations, if…" is much more likely to be correct than one that states the "process should be discontinued completely." The first is a calm rational statement and doesn't even make a definitive, uncompromising stance, using a hedge word *if* to provide wiggle room, whereas the second choice is far more extreme.

⊘ BENCHMARK

As you read through the answer choices and you come across one that seems to answer the question well, mentally select that answer choice. This is not your final answer, but it's the one that will help you evaluate the other answer choices. The one that you selected is your benchmark or standard for judging each of the other answer choices. Every other answer choice must be compared to your benchmark. That choice is correct until proven otherwise by another answer choice beating it. If you find a better answer, then that one becomes your new benchmark. Once you've decided that no other choice answers the question as well as your benchmark, you have your final answer.

⊘ PREDICT THE ANSWER

Before you even start looking at the answer choices, it is often best to try to predict the answer. When you come up with the answer on your own, it is easier to avoid distractions and traps because you will know exactly what to look for. The right answer choice is unlikely to be word-for-word what you came up with, but it should be a close match. Even if you are confident that you have the right answer, you should still take the time to read each option before moving on.

General Strategies

⊘ TOUGH QUESTIONS

If you are stumped on a problem or it appears too hard or too difficult, don't waste time. Move on! Remember though, if you can quickly check for obviously incorrect answer choices, your chances of guessing correctly are greatly improved. Before you completely give up, at least try to knock out a couple of possible answers. Eliminate what you can and then guess at the remaining answer choices before moving on.

⊘ CHECK YOUR WORK

Since you will probably not know every term listed and the answer to every question, it is important that you get credit for the ones that you do know. Don't miss any questions through careless mistakes. If at all possible, try to take a second to look back over your answer selection and make sure you've selected the correct answer choice and haven't made a costly careless mistake (such as marking an answer choice that you didn't mean to mark). This quick double check should more than pay for itself in caught mistakes for the time it costs.

⊘ PACE YOURSELF

It's easy to be overwhelmed when you're looking at a page full of questions; your mind is confused and full of random thoughts, and the clock is ticking down faster than you would like. Calm down and maintain the pace that you have set for yourself. Especially as you get down to the last few minutes of the test, don't let the small numbers on the clock make you panic. As long as you are on track by monitoring your pace, you are guaranteed to have time for each question.

⊘ DON'T RUSH

It is very easy to make errors when you are in a hurry. Maintaining a fast pace in answering questions is pointless if it makes you miss questions that you would have gotten right otherwise. Test writers like to include distracting information and wrong answers that seem right. Taking a little extra time to avoid careless mistakes can make all the difference in your test score. Find a pace that allows you to be confident in the answers that you select.

⊘ KEEP MOVING

Panicking will not help you pass the test, so do your best to stay calm and keep moving. Taking deep breaths and going through the answer elimination steps you practiced can help to break through a stress barrier and keep your pace.

Final Notes

The combination of a solid foundation of content knowledge and the confidence that comes from practicing your plan for applying that knowledge is the key to maximizing your performance on test day. As your foundation of content knowledge is built up and strengthened, you'll find that the strategies included in this chapter become more and more effective in helping you quickly sift through the distractions and traps of the test to isolate the correct answer.

Now that you're preparing to move forward into the test content chapters of this book, be sure to keep your goal in mind. As you read, think about how you will be able to apply this information on the test. If you've already seen sample questions for the test and you have an idea of the question format and style, try to come up with questions of your own that you can answer based on what you're reading. This will give you valuable practice applying your knowledge in the same ways you can expect to on test day.

Good luck and good studying!

Three-Week SIE Exam Study Plan

On the next few pages, we've provided an optional study plan to help you use this study guide to its fullest potential over the course of three weeks. If you have six weeks available and want to spread it out more, spend two weeks on each section of the plan.

Below is a quick summary of the subjects covered in each week of the plan.

- Week 1: Knowledge of Capital Markets & Understanding Products and Their Risks
- Week 2: Understanding Trading, Customer Accounts, and Prohibited Activities & Overview of the Regulatory Framework
- Week 3: Practice Tests

Please note that not all subjects will take the same amount of time to work through.

Three full-length practice tests are included in this study guide. We recommend saving the third test and any additional tests for after you've completed the study plan. Take these practice tests without any reference materials a day or two before the real thing as practice runs to get you in the mode of answering questions at a good pace.

Week 1: Knowledge of Capital Markets & Understanding Products and Their Risks

INSTRUCTIONAL CONTENT

First, read carefully through the Knowledge of Capital Markets & Understanding Products and Their Risks chapters in this book, checking off your progress as you go:

❑ Regulatory Entities, Agencies, and Market Participants
❑ Market Structure
❑ Economic Factors
❑ Offerings
❑ Products
❑ Investment Risks

As you read, do the following:

- Highlight any sections, terms, or concepts you think are important
- Draw an asterisk (*) next to any areas you are struggling with
- Watch the review videos to gain more understanding of a particular topic
- Take notes in your notebook or in the margins of this book

After you've read through everything, go back and review any sections that you highlighted or that you drew an asterisk next to, referencing your notes along the way.

Week 2: Understanding Trading, Customer Accounts, and Prohibited Activities & Overview of the Regulatory Framework

INSTRUCTIONAL CONTENT

First, read carefully through the Understanding Trading, Customer Accounts, and Prohibited Activities & Overview of the Regulatory Framework chapters in this book, checking off your progress as you go:

- ❏ Trading, Settlement, and Corporate Actions
- ❏ Customer Accounts and Compliance Considerations
- ❏ Prohibited Activities
- ❏ SRO Regulatory Requirements for Associated Persons
- ❏ Employee Conduct and Reportable Events

As you read, do the following:

- Highlight any sections, terms, or concepts you think are important
- Draw an asterisk (*) next to any areas you are struggling with
- Watch the review videos to gain more understanding of a particular topic
- Take notes in your notebook or in the margins of this book

After you've read through everything, go back and review any sections that you highlighted or that you drew an asterisk next to, referencing your notes along the way.

Week 3: Practice Tests

Your success on test day depends not only on how many hours you put into preparing, but also on whether you prepared the right way. It's good to check along the way to see if your studying is paying off. One of the most effective ways to do this is by taking practice tests to evaluate your progress. Practice tests are useful because they show exactly where you need to improve. Every time you take a practice test, pay special attention to these three groups of questions:

- The questions you got wrong
- The questions you had to guess on, even if you guessed right
- The questions you found difficult or slow to work through

This will show you exactly what your weak areas are, and where you need to devote more study time. Ask yourself why each of these questions gave you trouble. Was it because you didn't understand the material? Was it because you didn't remember the vocabulary? Do you need more repetitions on this type of question to build speed and confidence? Dig into those questions and figure out how you can strengthen your weak areas as you go back to review the material.

PRACTICE TEST #1

Now that you've read over the instructional content, it's time to take a practice test. Complete Practice Test #1. Take this test with **no time constraints**, and feel free to reference the applicable sections of this guide as you go. Once you've finished, check your answers against the provided answer key. For any questions you answered incorrectly, review the answer rationale, and then **go back and review** the applicable sections of the book. The goal in this stage is to understand why you answered the question incorrectly, and make sure that the next time you see a similar question, you will get it right.

PRACTICE TEST #2

Next, complete Practice Test #2. This time, give yourself **1 hour and 45 minutes** to complete all of the questions. You should again feel free to reference the guide and your notes, but be mindful of the clock. If you run out of time before you finish all of the questions, mark where you were when time expired, but go ahead and finish taking the practice test. Once you've finished, check your answers against the provided answer key, and as before, review the answer rationale for any that you answered incorrectly and then go back and review the associated instructional content. Your goal is still to increase understanding of the content but also to get used to the time constraints you will face on the test.

As you go along, keep in mind that the practice test is just that: practice. Memorizing these questions and answers will not be very helpful on the actual test because it is unlikely to have any of the same exact questions. If you only know the right answers to the sample questions, you won't be prepared for the real thing. **Study the concepts** until you understand them fully, and then you'll be able to answer any question that shows up on the test.

Knowledge of Capital Markets

Regulatory Entities, Agencies, and Market Participants

THE SECURITIES AND EXCHANGE COMMISSION (SEC)

THE HIGH-LEVEL PURPOSE AND MISSION OF SECURITIES REGULATION

The **Securities and Exchange Commission** was created in the wake of the 1929 stock market crash and the ensuing Great Depression. Up until that point, there was very little, if any, government involvement and regulation of the securities industry. This lack of oversight allowed many practices to take place in the securities markets that would be considered illegal by today's standards. The crash of '29 was partly due to the business practices of firms and investors leading up to that point. Post-1929, the federal government sought to increase oversight of the financial industry in order to prevent a crash of such magnitude from occurring ever again. This is what drove the creation and subsequent passing of the Securities Acts of 1933 and 1934, which created the Securities and Exchange Commission. The primary purpose of the SEC was and is primarily to protect **retail** investors in the public markets through the enforcement of various laws, rules, and regulations.

DEFINITION, JURISDICTION AND AUTHORITY OF THE SEC

The Securities Act of 1933, also known as the "**Prospectus**" or "**Paper**" Act, was passed by the United States Congress in response to the crash of 1929. Up until that point, the financial sector was seen as a "Wild West," with little to no regulation, oversight, or governance. The purpose of the Securities Act of '33 was to protect retail investors from fraud and theft in the securities market. The law took power from the states and invested it in the federal government. The most important provision in this law as it relates to the current financial markets is that it instituted the practice of corporations **registering with the SEC** via a **prospectus** document before issuing securities to the public, whether they be equity or debt securities (stocks or bonds). It is critical to remember that although corporations are required to register with the government before issuing shares to the public, the federal government and municipal governments are excluded from such registration requirements.

The Securities Act of 1934, also known as the "People and Places" Act, was a companion piece of legislation passed by Congress after the Securities Act of 1933. The primary purpose of the 1934 Act was to regulate the trading of securities on the **secondary market**. The secondary market is where securities trade after issue on the primary market, which is governed by the Securities Act of 1933. In addition to this, the legislation officially created the Securities and Exchange Commission, giving it full jurisdiction, interpretation, and authority over the laws governing the United States' domestic securities markets. All publicly traded corporations must abide by the rules set forth in '34 as it relates to the actions of the corporations, **broker-dealers**, investors, and financial professionals. This act helped to increase transparency and investor confidence through government enforcement via the SEC.

SELF-REGULATORY ORGANIZATIONS (SROS)

PURPOSE AND MISSION OF AN SRO

The **Financial Industry Regulatory Authority** was created by the merger of the National Association of Securities Dealers (NASD) and the regulatory arm of the **New York Stock Exchange** (NYSE). FINRA is the main **self-regulatory organization** (SRO) as it relates to the financial industry. The purpose of FINRA is to serve as just that, a regulatory entity for the securities

19

industry apart from the SEC. The four main standards that FINRA sets forth are the Code of Arbitration (final and binding arbitration for disputes), Code of Procedure (handles trade practice complaints), Code of Conduct (ethical behavior standard), and Uniform Practice Code (standardizes secondary market trading). These set the standards for financial professionals. It is important to note that the UPC states that **regular way settlement** for corporate and municipal bonds is T+2, and that they follow as 30-day month/360-day year. Regular way settlement for U.S. government securities is T+1 and is based on an actual/actual calendar.

The **Municipal Securities Rulemaking Board** (MSRB) is the SRO that oversees the municipal securities market (think **municipal bonds**) in the U.S. While the MSRB does set forth many rules and regulations for the industry, one of the most testable is rule G-37 "Campaign Contributions." This rule states that in order for a financial professional to contribute to a political campaign, they must (1) be able to vote for the candidate and (2) must not contribute more than $250 per election cycle. The **Chicago Board of Options Exchange** (CBOE) is another SRO that serves as the largest options exchange in the U.S. They provide options for many listed securities, including individual stocks, indices, and exchange-traded funds. There are no applicable rules set forth by the CBOE that one must know for the SIE Exam.

OTHER REGULATORS AND AGENCIES
DEPARTMENT OF THE TREASURY/IRS

The **Financial Crimes Enforcement Network** (FINCEN) is a bureau within the U.S. Department of the Treasury. Under the "**Bank Secrecy Act**" (The Currency and Foreign Transactions Reporting Act of 1970), banks and financial institutions file **Currency Transaction Reports** (CTRs) and **Suspicious Activity Reports** (SARs). CTRs are filed with FINCEN by institutions when they process currency transactions in excess of $10,000. SARs are filed by institutions whenever they receive a transaction that is deemed "commercially illogical." The purpose of this framework is to prevent money laundering. It is important to remember that money laundering consists of three phases: placement, layering, and integration. This is the process that takes "dirty money" and turns it into "clean money" that is unidentifiable by the IRS. There is also the practice of "structuring," where individuals will try to avoid triggering a CTR filing by breaking up transactions into smaller amounts.

The **North American Securities Administrators Association** (NASAA) is an organization comprised of **state administrators**. It is important to note that the financial industry is regulated by both the federal and state governments, which is where NASAA links up with SROs such as FINRA. The 60 Series licenses that many investments professional take after the SIE and Series 6/7 are NASAA exams that detail how to file securities with state administrators. Not all rules are consistent from state to state, which is why firms must take care to abide by the regulations set forth by the state administrator or regulator. The laws that govern the registration, offering, and sale of securities within states are referred to as "blue sky laws." The purpose of NASAA and "blue sky laws" is primarily to protect retail investors from fraud and deception in capital markets.

THE FEDERAL RESERVE

The Federal Reserve is a massive force in the U.S. economy, and for the SIE it is critical to remember that the Federal Reserve tells banks how much they must keep in their tills in reserve against their liabilities (reserve requirements), and how much they can lend to other depository institutions overnight, referred to as the (Federal Funds Rate). These exist partly in response to the stock market crash of 1929, when overleveraged banks collapsed as individuals made a run to cash out their accounts and the economy crashed. The Federal Reserve is also responsible for Regulation T, which oversees the borrowing and credit extension practices of broker-dealers. This power was

originally maintained by the firms themselves until the Securities Act of 1934 gave that power to the Federal Reserve. This helps to ensure fairness and standardization across the industry.

FEDERAL DEPOSIT INSURANCE CORPORATION (FDIC)

The Federal Deposit Insurance Corporation (FDIC) was established by the federal government in order to help back financial institutions and secure individual accounts. The FDIC covers normal bank accounts such as checking and savings accounts up to $250,000. This means that $250,000 of what is in a person's bank account is backed by the full faith of the federal government. This also works for multiple accounts as long as they are registered with different financial institutions, not simply different branches of the same bank. The **Securities Investor Protection Corporation** (SIPC) accomplishes a similar role for investment accounts. SIPC will cover an individual's investment account up to $500,000, of which no more than $250,000 will be covered in cash, the rest to be covered in securities. This is useful in the case that a broker-dealer goes bankrupt and is unable to deliver shares to their clients. In this case, SIPC could liquidate the firm and then attempt to cover the investor's balances with the proceeds from the liquidation.

MARKET PARTICIPANTS AND THEIR ROLES

INVESTORS

The majority of investors in the market are considered retail investors, meaning they are not professionals. An investor can become an accredited investor by meeting one of three eligibility requirements:

- annual income in excess of $200,000 per year for the past two years with reasonable expectation for the same this year
- if married, joint annual income in excess of $300,000 per year for the past two years with reasonable expectation for the same this year
- a net worth in excess of $1 million, excluding primary residence.

Accredited investors have access to private investments that are not open to the public. The reason for this is the government views retail investors as more vulnerable to fraud and loss of investments, but see accredited investors as able to financially survive large or even total losses on certain investment vehicles.

An **institutional investor** refers to corporations, pension funds, governments, and other organizations that buy and sell securities. If the investor is a non-natural person, it is an institutional investor. There are also what are referred to as **Qualified Institutional Buyers**. These are institutional investors that own or manage a minimum of $100 million worth of securities. Not all institutional investors are QIBs, but all QIBs are institutional investors. The SEC regards these entities as "sophisticated investors," similar to accredited investors. They are offered the ability to invest in non-registered securities such as **private placements** and **PIPEs** (private investment in a public company). This goes back to the idea that unregistered securities carry more risk, and therefore retail investors (who stand to lose a greater percentage of their total net worth) are not allowed to participate.

BROKER-DEALERS

Broker-dealers are the firms that sell and help to facilitate the sale of securities on the secondary market. A clearing firm is made up of different departments, such as order, purchase and sales, margin, and cashiering. They manage the confirmation, settlement, and delivery of equity transactions. An introducing firm will show a customer to a clearing firm. This takes place when a smaller broker-dealer does not have the capacity to act as a clearing firm. Finally, prime brokers are firms that provide custody and financing for **hedge funds**.

INVESTMENT ADVISERS

Investment advisors are financial professionals that sell their advice as a service to clients and are usually compensated in the form of a fee. A simple test to determine whether someone is an investment advisor is the ABC test: Advice, Business, Compensation. If a firm or individual is offering advice as their business model and is receiving compensation for their advice, then they are an investment advisor. Investment advisors come in many forms and can fill diverse roles such as wealth management, retirement planning, estate planning, funds management, and general advice.

MUNICIPAL ADVISORS

Municipal advisors are professionals that advise municipalities on the issue of securities. These issuers include state, local, and city governments, among other entities. It is important to note that the municipal debt market is a very large part of the overall U.S. debt market alongside corporate and U.S. government debt securities. Therefore, this is a very important role. Due to the potential

22

conflict of interest that could arise, municipal advisors are not allowed to switch from advisor to **underwriter** for a client. This way, the advisor could not structure a deal that would be unfairly advantageous to themselves.

ISSUERS AND UNDERWRITERS

Issuers are entities that wish to sell securities to the public. These entities can take the form of corporations or governments. The securities could be either equity securities in the form of common or preferred stock, or debt securities in the form of bonds. The issuer is the firm that receives payment for the sale of securities on the **primary market**. The underwriter is the firm the issuer hires to facilitate the transaction and actually complete the sale to the public. The underwriter handles the issuing, keeps track of the registrations, and forms an underwriting syndicate of other firms to assist in the issue. The issuer pays a fee to the underwriter in exchange for these services. Underwriting is very lucrative and is usually managed by top investment banks, such as Goldman Sachs, J.P. Morgan, and Morgan Stanley.

TRADERS AND MARKET MAKERS

Traders refers to the firms and individuals on the trading floor of exchanges such as the NYSE. These individuals buy and sell securities in line with their investment firm's wishes. Market makers are large firms that provide liquidity in the market. The way they accomplish this is by buying at the "bid" and selling at the "ask." Keep in mind that when an investor wants to purchase a security, they purchase at the ask price and sell at the bid price. This is how market makers make their money off the "spread", the difference between the bid and ask prices. Although this may be a difference of only $0.05 depending on the security, it can become a large sum when the market maker is buying and selling tens of thousands of shares.

CUSTODIANS, TRUSTEES, AND TRANSFER AGENTS

A custodian is a firm that controls or safeguards securities for an individual and sometimes takes an active role in the management of those securities. Trustees fill a similar role to trustees in the legal sense: they act on behalf of beneficiaries, usually in the areas of pension and retirement plans, bankruptcies, and other financial events. Transfer agents facilitate a change in ownership by canceling old shares and issuing new ones to buyers in the secondary market. These transfer agents work alongside a firm's registrar or bookkeepers to keep track of who owns the shares, how much they own, etc. This ensures that people are on the list for important events and disclosures such information as proxies and board meetings.

DEPOSITORIES AND CLEARING CORPORATIONS

Depositories and clearing corporations, such as the Depository Trust & Clearing Corporation (DTCC), and the Options Clearing Corporation (OCC), serve as issuers and guarantors in the market. For example, the OCC serves as the issuer and guarantor of all options. This means that you do not have to worry that the person on the other side of an option contract will live up to their side of the exchange—the OCC ensures that the deal happens in the manner it was agreed upon. This is helpful for investors as it eliminates a level of risk in options trading. The OCC is the only testable depository and clearing corporation for the purposes of the SIE Exam.

Market Structure

TYPES OF MARKETS
THE PRIMARY MARKET

The primary market is the market where issuers sell new securities to the public, usually with the aid of an underwriter. This is where new bonds and corporate paper are sold to the public, as well as Initial Public Offerings (IPOs). When a corporation wants to sell new securities (issued but not yet outstanding shares), they will hire an underwriter to structure the deal and facilitate the transactions. This serves as a source of funding for the company and a source of fee income for the underwriters. After shares are purchased on the primary market, they are then sold on the secondary market. It is important to note that certain securities trade only on the primary market, which means they can only be bought and sold from the issuer. This umbrella includes certain mutual funds as well as U.S. government treasury debt.

THE SECONDARY MARKET

The secondary market is the market in which the previous owner receives the proceeds of the sale of securities. When an investor purchases shares of a company through their brokerage platform, that sale takes place on the secondary market; the shares are being purchased from another investor who is selling their shares, rather than directly from the issuer themselves. The NYSE and Nasdaq are examples of the secondary market. These securities can be traded on an electronic, over-the-counter (OTC), or physical basis.

THE THIRD MARKET

The third market is where investors and institutions trade securities on an OTC basis rather than through a listed exchange such as the NYSE. It is important to note that the securities being traded in the third market are exchange-listed (meaning they can be purchased on the secondary market as well), but here they trade on an OTC basis on a broker-dealer network rather than through the exchanges. This is what differentiates the third market from the secondary market. The third market attracts large investors like investment firms and pension funds since there are no broker fees, which leads to lower prices for the firms.

THE FOURTH MARKET

The fourth market is the final type of market in the securities industry and refers to private OTC trades between institutions. The fourth market shares similarities with the third market in that the trades are OTC, but unlike the third market, there are no broker-dealers involved. This allows institutions to directly exchange large amounts of securities between one another without intermediaries and without moving the market. The fourth market is a subject of concern for some investors as it allows very large firms to trade massive quantities of shares and derivatives with anonymity.

Economic Factors

THE FEDERAL RESERVE BOARD'S IMPACT ON BUSINESS ACTIVITY AND MARKET STABILITY

MONETARY VS. FISCAL POLICY

Monetary policy refers to the money supply and is controlled by the Federal Reserve. FED interest rates are an example of monetary policy, as are the discount and federal funds rates. Fiscal policy refers to taxation and government spending and is therefore controlled by the U.S. Congress and President. Fiscal policy has a large impact on the economy because the United States government spending makes up a significant amount of GDP, and taxation is a large source of revenue for the federal government. Both monetary and fiscal policy are tools that the government uses to influence the money supply.

OPEN MARKET ACTIVITIES AND IMPACT ON ECONOMY

In a market economy such as the United States, there exists a complex exchange between many independent variables that affect the overall economy. Some examples include inflation and GDP. Inflation is simply defined as too much money chasing too few goods. This is where demand for goods outpaces the supply. Deflation is where too little money is chasing too many goods. Here, the demand for goods is too low to meet the supply. Usually, the more money that is pumped into the economy through quantitative easing or an increase in borrowing, the higher inflation climbs in response. Gross Domestic Product is a tool used to measure the output of an economy. There are many different types of GDP, such as real GDP, nominal GDP, actual GDP, and potential GDP. Something important to note about GDP is that two quarters of declining GDP meets the definition for a recession, whereas six quarters of declining GDP or a severe drop in GDP meets the definition for a depression.

RATES SET BY THE FED

The Federal Reserve (FED) controls monetary policy and sets various rates that directly and indirectly influence the economy. The interest rate refers to the cost to borrow money. This is set by the Federal Open Market Committee (FOMC) in the United States. If the government desires to tighten the money supply to curb inflation or similar, they will raise interest rates to increase the cost of capital and therefore decrease borrowing and spending, thus cooling inflation. The prime rate refers to the rate that banks will charge their customers with the highest credit ratings. The discount rate is the rate that the FED charges banks when they borrow funds from a Federal Reserve bank. This is set directly by the FED. The federal funds rate is the rate at which banks charge one another for overnight loans. Note that this rate is not set by the FED, but rather the actual fed funds rate is in between a maximum and minimum rate bracket that the FED will set.

BUSINESS ECONOMIC FACTORS

FINANCIAL STATEMENTS

The income statement (also referred to as the profit and loss statement or P&L) is a financial statement that tells a company how much money they made in a given period (usually a quarterly or annual basis). To give a simple example, an income statement starts with total revenue, subtracts cost of goods sold to deliver the gross profit, then subtracts any selling, general and administrative expenses to yield the operating profit. The operating profit is also known as earnings before interest, tax, depreciation, and amortization (EBITDA), and is a key number used in valuation multiples for enterprise value. Once operating profit has been reached, any interest, expenses, depreciation, and amortization are taken out. Then subtract income tax for the corporation to deliver the final number: net income. Net income is the take-home money the firm has after everything is paid for. Net income is either paid out in the form of dividends or reinvested into the business. Net income flows into retained earnings on the statement of retained earnings and increases the cash balance of the firm on the balance sheet.

The balance sheet is a snapshot of the business at any given time. It shows the assets, liabilities, and equity of a business. The accounting equation is the backbone of the balance sheet and is essential to remember. The accounting equation is Assets equals Liabilities plus Equity ($A = L + E$). This is why it is called a balance sheet: the assets must always equal the liabilities plus the equity. hence the "balance." Remember, assets are things that generate revenue for the business, such as cash and securities, receivables, property, plant, and equipment, etc. Liabilities are items that require something from the business, usually in the form of a payment or cash outflow. These include accounts payable, debts, etc. Equity refers to the investment on the part of owners into the business. Shares of the company make up the equity, hence the term equity securities, which refers to stock that is sold in the market or held privately. When you buy a share, you are buying a portion of the company.

The statement of cash flows is divided into three sections: operating activities, investing activities, and financing activities. Operating activities simply refers to the operations of the business that generate sales and cashflow. A company that does not have positive operating cashflows will most likely not be a company for long. Negative operating cash flows means that they are losing money on their operations as a firm. Investing activities refers to investments that the business makes, such as CAPEX (capital expenditures), investments into securities, and therefore the sale of said equipment and securities. Financing activities are composed of the issuance of new debt or equity, as well as the payment of existing debt, whether it be loans from a bank or corporate debt that the company sold. The cash received from financing would be an inflow, whereas the payments on the existing debt would be an outflow.

A public company must be registered with the SEC per the Securities Act of 1934. A public company is required to release financial statements quarterly and annually. The company will file what is called a form 10-Q with the SEC on a quarterly basis, and a 10-K on an annual basis. These are the financial statements that investors review when analyzing a company for a potential investment. There are various other forms that a public company must register with the SEC, such as prospectuses, notices of insider trading, and many others. The most important to remember are the company's 10-Qs and 10-Ks.

BUSINESS CYCLE

The business cycle refers to the different highs and lows that the economy experiences at any given time. A contraction in the business cycle refers to a point at which the economy is declining. After a contraction, the business cycle normally enters a phase known as a trough. This refers to the point in which the business cycle has stopped declining from the contraction but stays stagnant and growth stays flat, hence the name "trough." Expansion is just that: the economy expanding. An expansion will normally lead to a peak in the business cycle which is then followed by a contraction, and the cycle perpetuates itself.

PERFORMANCE INDICATORS

There are many indicators in the stock market that professionals use to gauge the performance of a company. Leading indicators are tools that point toward future events. An example would be bond yields, which can serve as a leading indicator for the stock market. Remember, indication does not equal certainty. Indicators may point towards a given event, but there is no certainty that the event will actually transpire. Lagging indicators are indicators that are looked at after an event. They are used to confirm a pattern that has been played out. Examples include CPI and the unemployment

rate. Finally, coincident indicators are indicators that play out during an event that they track. They are concurrent to the event. A few examples of concurrent indicators would be both GDP and personal income.

BOND AND EQUITY MARKETS

A cyclical company is one whose stock price tends to follow the business cycle (i.e., appreciating in value during expansion and declining in value during contraction). Cyclical companies sell goods or services that are non-essential, meaning that people will decrease their purchasing if the economy tightens. Examples include construction, real estate, and consumer cyclical companies like entertainment and retail. Defensive stocks are the opposite of cyclical: they are resilient to the business cycle and sell goods or services that stay strong even during a contraction in the economy. Examples of defensive stocks include energy companies, food, etc. Finally, growth companies are firms where excess cash is used to finance expansion, leading to an appreciation in the value of the underlying stock price. This is in contrast to dividend stocks, where excess cash is paid out in the form of a dividend to the shareholders. Growth stocks tend to be more aggressive, whereas dividend stocks tend to be more risk-averse and cemented within their industry. Typically, a recession is a time to be in bonds and an expansion is a time to be in stocks, but this is not always the case.

PRINCIPAL ECONOMIC THEORIES

The Keynesian school of thought is named after Sir John Maynard Keynes who led the movement. Keynesian economics holds to the idea that government spending and taxation should be used as tools in the economy that can positively impact the business cycle. An example of this would be the government increasing taxes to cool off the economy or vice versa. In comparison to this theory, the Monetarists believe that the government should use the FED to control the money supply to affect the business cycle. An example of this would be the FED using quantitative easing (a monetary policy) to purchase securities in the open market, adding them to the balance sheet and thus injecting money into the economy. These two theories are not mutually exclusive, and governments will usually use tools from both theories when attempting to effectuate change in the economy.

INTERNATIONAL ECONOMIC FACTORS
U.S. BALANCE OF PAYMENTS

The balance of payments refers to the trade that takes place between countries and the balance between foreign and domestic currencies. Economists will refer to one currency as being "strong" against another. What this means is that the strong currency has increased buying power as compared to the "weak" currency. This is reflected in countries where the cost of living in terms of USD is extremely low. This is partly because the USD is much stronger than the host currency. Other traditionally strong currencies include the British Pound Sterling, the Euro, the Swiss Franc, and several others.

GROSS DOMESTIC PRODUCT (GDP) AND GROSS NATIONAL PRODUCT (GNP)

Gross Domestic Product (GDP) refers to the total output of an economy. This is measured by including the value of the final goods and services in the market. GDP can get quite convoluted as an economy is a very complex machine, but what is important to remember is that GDP is primarily made up of consumer spending, government spending, business investment, and exports and imports. All these together make up the GDP. The larger a country's GDP, the larger its economy. Some U.S. states (e.g., California, Texas, and Florida) have economies that, if they were to be countries themselves, would be in the top 10 largest economies in the world. Gross National Product is defined as the final value of finished domestic goods and services owned by the citizens of a country, whether the goods were produced in the host country or not. GNP can be either higher or lower than GDP depending on whether the income residents make in foreign countries is less than what is earned by foreign residents. Both GDP and GNP are tools for measuring an economy in the aggregate.

EXCHANGE RATES

The spot rate is the current exchange rate between two currencies. For instance, the spot rate between the USD and the Euro at any given point might be 1:1.01, the next day it could be 1:1.02. The spot rate changes and fluctuates with the rest of the foreign currencies. This spot rate serves as the foundation for forex (foreign exchange) trading. This is where investors "bet" on one currency getting weaker or stronger against another. This is all based on the spot rate. A pertinent example of this would be forex traders who bet on the USD against the Russian Ruble prior to Russia's invasion of Ukraine in the early part of 2022. The Ruble weakened significantly against the U.S. dollar, and the investors who had locked in those trades prior to the movement made a considerable return. Forex trading is a very complicated and risky business, but all you need to remember for the SIE is that the spot exchange rate is the current exchange rate between any two given currencies at any given time.

Offerings

ROLES OF PARTICIPANTS

When a company wants to issue shares to the public on the primary market, it will hire an investment bank as an underwriter to help with the sale of the securities. The underwriter will typically outsource some of the workloads to other investment banks, thus forming the underwriting syndicate. The lead underwriter is the one the issuer pays, and the lead underwriter then pays a portion of the fee out to the members of the syndicate. Investment banking can be very lucrative, especially off large IPOs. Large investment banks like Morgan Stanley, J.P. Morgan, and Goldman Sachs are some of the most prestigious names in the industry, and therefore usually get their pick of deals for underwriting. This arrangement allows the issuer to focus on running the company while the underwriter takes care of the sale of securities. In a municipal setting, a municipal advisor may advise on the selling of debt securities to the public but may not serve as both advisor and underwriter, as this would create a conflict of interest.

TYPES OF OFFERINGS

In accordance with the Securities Acts of 1933 and 1934, all public securities must be registered with the SEC. This is a painstaking and laborious process that many firms choose to avoid until necessary for the growth of the company. A public offering is referred to as an Initial Public Offering (IPO) and is managed by an underwriter who helps sell the shares to the public. A private securities offering can only be offered to accredited investors who meet the SEC's income or net worth requirements. This would include institutional investors and high-income-earning individuals. These private offerings are usually referred to as Private Investments in a Public Enterprise (PIPE).

INITIAL PUBLIC OFFERING (IPO), SECONDARY OFFERING, AND FOLLOW-ON OFFERING

IPOs are the initial public offering that a firm makes to the public. This IPO is made up of shares that are authorized by the firm's charter but not yet outstanding. Once outstanding they are factored into the company's market capitalization, which is calculated by multiplying the firm's stock price by the total number of shares outstanding. If a company chooses to buy back shares, which they may do if they feel the share price is undervalued, those reacquired shares will enter the corporate treasury and thus are known as treasury stock. A secondary offering takes place after the IPO and refers to when an investor sells their shares on the secondary market. Remember, the secondary market is where the previous owner receives the proceeds of the sale, not the issuer. A company can also complete a follow-on offering. This is where the corporation issues new shares to the public and is sometimes referred to as a secondary offering as well. This can be either a dilutive offering (which results in an increase in total shares) or non-dilutive (which results in no new shares being issued).

METHODS OF DISTRIBUTION

Not all public offerings have the same methods of distribution. The underwriter can take on different levels of responsibility in the offering. A best-efforts distribution is where the underwriter does their best to sell as much of the stock as possible but has no liability for any unsold shares. This is an important concept—when a company issues shares, unless there is a firm commitment on the part of the underwriter, they have no guarantee that all the shares will be sold. A firm commitment is where the underwriter promises to purchase any unsold securities. This is a liability for the underwriter, as any unsold securities will have to be purchased by the underwriter.

SHELF REGISTRATIONS AND DISTRIBUTIONS

When a company registers shares, not all must be issued and sold to the public. In certain instances, the company will "shelve" securities by registering them, but not selling them to the public. This allows those shelved securities to be used in mergers and acquisitions where the firm wishes to use its own stock as a form of payment. This is very common amongst large companies. These shelf registrations can also be taken from follow-on offerings. Shelved securities are good for two to three years depending on the issuer. All this does is save time and money for the issuer. If they wish to issue more shares down the road, they can take them from the shelf rather than having to register new shares with the SEC.

TYPES AND PURPOSE OF OFFERING DOCUMENTS AND DELIVERY REQUIREMENTS

When a corporation or government wants to issue securities (whether they be equity or debt) there are certain documents that must be created and disclosed. In a municipal bond setting, this is referred to as an official statement (remember that municipal bonds are exempt from registration with the SEC under the Securities Act of 1934). Under Reg D with a PIPE, the issuer must make available a private placement memorandum. In a public offering, the issuer must create a prospectus. Both the private placement memorandum and the prospectus are forms of program disclosure documents. Remember that issuers are also beholden to state administrators under blue sky laws.

REGULATORY FILING REQUIREMENTS AND EXEMPTIONS

Governments (both municipal, state, and federal) are exempt from registration with the SEC. Corporations do not receive the same treatment. Some corporations choose to get around registration with the SEC through private investments, though the opportunity for cash is not as great as it is in a public offering set. Issuers are required to clear their securities through their state administrator under the blue-sky laws of the state. The North American Securities Administrators Association (NASAA) is the SRO that helps to oversee these laws and their enforcement. The issuer must make the state administrator aware of the new issue through either coordination, notification, or qualification. This duality between federal and state governments creates an extra level of complexity for offerings. This is why securities industry professionals are required to take a Series 63, 65, or 66 (which cover NASAA and state laws) after passing the Series 6 or 7.

Understanding Products and Their Risks

Products

EQUITY SECURITIES

COMMON STOCK

Common stock is a form of equity in a company that can be listed on a stock exchange like the NYSE. Common stock gives the owner partial ownership in the company. Common stockholders are therefore considered "owners" of a company, which means they would be last in line to receive their money back in the event of a bankruptcy filing. Since stockholders are considered owners rather than creditors (debt holders or bond holders), they are entitled to certain rights of ownership. Among these rights of ownership are the right to inspect statements and documents (like annual financials); the right to vote on company decisions (board meetings); the ability to transfer ownership to another party (e.g., selling in the secondary market); dividend rights (if declared by the board); and the ability to sue for malfeasance or fraud. Companies send financial statements and proxies to common stockholders, though they are available online for anyone to view. It is important to remember that common stockholders are not guaranteed a dividend—they only have a right to a dividend if declared by the board of directors. Common stock is what people are normally referring too when they talk about shares of a company that trade in the secondary market.

PREFERRED STOCK

Preferred stock is different to common stock in that it is denominated out of a par value, such as $100, and is purchased directly from the company. These are a suitable option for institutional investors. Preferred stockholders cannot vote, and their shares do not appreciate in the market. If a dividend is declared, then preferred stockholders must be paid prior to common stockholders and are usually paid a higher distribution than their common counterpart. Preferred stockholders are also in front of common stockholders in the event of company liquidation. Some preferred stock has special privileges that force companies to pay preferred shareholders before common shareholders if they missed payments in prior years. These are considered dividends in arrears and mean that preferred shareholders will always get the first distribution. There are four main special forms of preferred stock: callable, convertible, cumulative, and participating.

Callable preferred stock is a unique form of preferred shares that can be called back by the issuing company when they see fit. This is referred to as a call provision and exists in the bond market as well. A company would do this is if interest rates fall and they realize they could call their preferred shares back and reissue them at a lower rate. It would not make sense for a company to keep paying higher than market average to their preferred shareholders if they do not have to. If a preferred share does not have this option however, than the company cannot call it back. The opposite of a call provision would be a put provision, where the holder can "put" the security back to the issuer.

Convertible preferred stock is preferred stock that can be converted into the company's common stock. This special privilege normally carries with it a lower yield. A preferred shareholder would convert their shares into common stock if the conversion price they secured with their preferred shares is below the current market price of the common stock. There is a conversion price as well as conversion ratio that are factored into this equation. The option to convert is attractive to many

31

preferred shareholders, as it allows them to take advantage of capital appreciation in the market for common stock.

Cumulative preferred stock is the kind that has a right to unpaid dividends. This means if a company fails to pay their full dividend amount to preferred shareholders one year, they must pay back the preferred shareholders before paying a cent to common shareholders. This is attractive to preferred shareholders because it ensures preferential treatment for income, which is normally the investment objective of preferred shareholders. This is contrasted with common stockholders, who are more focused on capital appreciation (usually).

Participating preferred stock is preferred stock that has the added benefit of voting rights in elections. This means preferred stockholders can also vote for board of directors and other company decisions similar to common shareholders. Corporate voting can take two forms: cumulative voting or statutory. Cumulative voting allows minority shareholders to have greater influence compared to statutory voting. If there are three board vacancies, a shareholder might receive 100 votes per seat. Under statutory voting, they may only place 100 votes per seat, but under cumulative voting they could place all 300 on a single position if they so desired.

RIGHTS

Rights are a form of equity security that are normally offered to existing shareholders. They are sometimes used to "sweeten" a deal when a company dilutes their shares by offering new shares to the public. Rights typically will only be able to purchase a fraction of a share, so many rights are needed to convert into a single share. Sometimes the company will offer rights to existing shareholders that can be exercised and converted into common stock which allows them to maintain proportional ownership. Rights usually have an exercise price below the current market price of the stock and are short-term instruments; they typically expire in 30-60 days after they are issued. Rights are contrasted with warrants.

WARRANTS

Warrants are similar to rights in that they are typically offered to existing shareholders. They are longer term instruments and typically cannot be exercised until 6-12 months after they are offered. They have a strike price that is above the current market price which means that the holder will wait until the market price of the shares exceeds the exercise price before exercising in order to lock in a gain. Warrants are sometime added onto bonds or preferred stocks as a "sweetener."

AMERICAN DEPOSITARY RECEIPTS (ADRs)

American Depositary Receipts are a type of equity security. They are foreign securities that are repackaged in order to be sold on a domestic U.S. stock exchange. If a U.S. investor wants to buy shares in a foreign company through their U.S. broker, they would be buying an ADR. It is important to remember that ADRs expose the investor to foreign exchange and political risk as dividends are normally paid in the foreign currency before being converted into U.S. dollars. Investors can also choose to place money in international stock funds through a mutual fund or ETFs.

OWNERSHIP

The order of liquidation refers to who gets their money first if a company restructures or enters into bankruptcy. First up would be secured bondholders; they have the first dibs on proceeds from the sale of assets. After secured bondholders would be subordinated or unsecured bondholders. Both secured and unsecured bondholders are creditors of the company, since they hold debt. After creditors comes owners in the form of preferred and common stockholders. Preferred stockholders are placed above common, since higher claim to assets is one of the "preferred" rights. Last comes

common stockholders, if there is anything left. When **long** on a position, whether it be bonds or stocks, the investor can only lose what they put in. When **short** on a position, the investor is subject to unlimited risk and loss potential. Most companies have limited liability, meaning owners and investors can only lose what they put it and their personal assets stay separate from the company.

VOTING RIGHTS

Common stockholders have greater voting privileges than preferred stockholders. Unless the preferred stock is "participating", it generally carries no voting rights. Shareholders can vote on board of directors as well as any decision that would affect their ownership in the company, such as a stock splits or proposed mergers and acquisitions, as well as administrative items. Shareholders can attend board meetings to vote or vote through proxies. The two types of voting are statutory and cumulative voting. Statutory voting is where the investor can only vote a limited amount on each position for the board, whereas cumulative voting allows the investor to put all their votes on a single position if they so desire. Cumulative voting gives greater power to minority shareholders as they can put greater weight on one position rather than spreading it out amongst many positions.

CONVERTIBLE SECURITIES

Convertible securities can be converted into a different type of asset. Usually, this comes in the form of convertible preferred stock or convertible bonds. Preferred stock that is convertible into common stock allows the holder the option to trade their preferred stock for common stock. This gives the investor access to the market appreciation of common stock (remember, preferred stock delivers income but no capital appreciation). Convertible bonds are issued by corporations and can be converted into the issuer's common stock at the discretion of the bondholder. This has a similar function to convertible preferred shares. It is important to remember the conversion price as well as the conversion ratio when dealing with convertible securities. The conversion ratio is usually found by taking the par value of the stock or bonds and dividing it by the market price of the shares.

CONTROL AND RESTRICTIONS

A controlled person is anyone who is considered an insider of the corporation. This can include officers, directors, and principal stockholders who control more than 10% of the outstanding stock. These individuals are subject to restrictions on how and when they can sell their shares. Rule 144 says that a controlled person can only sell 1% of the outstanding stock or the average of the last four weeks trading volume, whichever is greater. This can be done every 90 days (effectively four times per year). A form 144 must be filed at or prior to the sale of these securities. The shares these controlled persons hold could be either outstanding or not, but it is restricted either way.

33

DEBT INSTRUMENTS
TREASURY SECURITIES

Treasury bills are a short-term debt instrument issued by the United States government. They have zero default risk as they are covered by the full faith and credit of the U.S. government. T-Bills have maturities that range from a few days to 52 weeks at most. They are sold at a discount to par. When the bond matures at par you will make the difference between the discount price and the par value, which will be your interest. The discount rate is determined at auction and the minimum purchase amount is $100. T-Bills are a good short-term debt security with minimal risk.

Treasury notes are the next step up for U.S. gov securities. They have maturities ranging from two to ten years, making them an intermediate-term instrument. They are issued in maturities of two, three, five, seven, and ten years. They trade directly from the Treasury but also have an active secondary market which helps to provide liquidity. They can be purchased on either a noncompetitive bid or competitive bid basis. T-Notes earn a fixed rate of interest semi-annually (every six months), like most government securities. They have a minimum purchase amount of $100, similar to T-Bills. T-Notes are suitable for investors who are looking for safety of principle and income. Remember that the further the maturity on a bond, the higher the interest rate risk, meaning if interest rates change and the note you currently hold is now paying less than the market interest rate, you are losing out on those gains.

Treasury receipts, aka Separate Trading of Registered Interest and Principal of Securities (STRIPS), are issued by the corporations at a discount to par and mature at par value. This is one of many zero-coupon bonds. Remember that the coupon on a bond is just another way of saying the interest that it pays. Similar to T-Bills, treasury receipts pay no interest. Treasury receipts are not issued by the Treasury, but they are backed by T-Bonds. What happens is a corporation buys up bonds and strips them down into principal and interest payments. The principal amounts are then wrapped up and sold individually to investors, hence the treasury receipt. They are collateralized by T-Bonds, making them a safer investment, though they are not technically backed by the government.

TIPS and STRIPS are two unique forms of Treasury securities. Treasury Inflation-Protected Securities (TIPS) are T-Bonds whose interest and principal payments will be adjusted based on CPI readings. This effectively eliminates purchasing power risk for investors, as they will earn more when inflation is high and less when it is low. This is a type of security similar to Series I bonds that are also adjusted for inflation.

T-Bonds are long-term debt instruments issued by the United States government. They are issued with 10-to-30-year maturities and pay a fixed coupon every six months just like T-Notes. They follow the same minimum investment of $100, and their yield is determined at auction. Due to the way bond prices and interest rates work, bonds with longer maturities tend to be more volatile than those with shorter maturities. Since T-Bonds are backed by the government's ability to tax its citizens, they are virtually risk-free. However, that usually means investors will receive a lower interest payment for that safety. Corporate bonds can pay higher interest in order to attract investors as they are inherently more risky.

US AGENCIES

There are several U.S. agencies that issue debt and sell securities to the public. There is the Government National Mortgage Association (Ginnie Mae), the Federal National Mortgage Association (Fannie Mae), the Federal Home Loan Mortgage Corporation (Freddie Mac), and the Student Loan Marketing Association (Sallie Mae). The first three mainly deal in mortgage-backed securities like collateralized mortgage obligations (CMOs) which can be broken down into PACs,

TACs, and plain vanilla tranches. The important thing to remember here is that Ginnie Mae is the only agency that is fully backed by the faith and credit of the government; the rest are only implicitly backed. This goes back to the fallout of the Great Financial Crisis and the bailouts and spinoffs the government and large banks had to engage in to keep the economy afloat.

A mortgage-backed security (MBS) is a type of asset-backed security that is a popular investment in the financial world. These derivatives were one of the key factors that led to the Great Financial Crisis and crash of '08. There are different types of MBSs, such as collateralized mortgage obligations (CMOs). These securities can be divided into different tranches such as companion tranches, vanilla tranches, PACs and TACs. These will be covered in more depth on the Series 7 top off. Remember that mortgages are secured loans, as the property serves as backing for the loan. This can make MBSs a relatively safe investment unless the mortgages are sub-prime (which was the issue leading up to '08).

CORPORATE BONDS

Corporations issue debt in order to raise capital for new ventures. The two main ways a company can attain financing are through selling bonds in order to raise debt or selling shares in order to raise equity. Corporations can issue either secured or unsecured debt. Secured debt is usually backed by an asset, like equipment, whereas unsecured is not. Mortgages are an example of a secured debt (asset-backed). Remember that secured debt holders take priority in liquidation. Debentures is another name for corporation's unsecured debt. They are riskier than secured and therefore can carry higher yields. Bonds are rated mainly by the two large rating agencies in the U.S.: S&P and Moody's. They have similar ratings, with AAA being the highest rating for S&P and Aaa being the highest for Moody's. Anything below BBB or Baa is considered a "junk" bond and is not investment grade. Usually, investors will want to steer clear of junk debt. Corporations can also issue bonds with many features such as convertible or callable bonds. These have similar functions to the ones found in preferred stock.

MUNICIPAL SECURITIES

Besides the treasury and corporations, municipalities make up the greatest amount of the bond market. These include states as well as local governments and jurisdictions. "Munies" carry unique characteristics and are sometimes excluded from tax at the federal level, making them very attractive to wealthy investors. The MSRB is the regulatory authority that oversees the actions of financial institutions in this field. There are many specific types of "Munies", including GOs, Revenue bonds, Special Purpose bonds, etc. These carry unique tax implications depending on the interest and capital gains.

GENERAL OBLIGATION (GO) BONDS

General obligation bonds are issued by municipalities to pay for various needs that the community has. It is backed by the creditworthiness of the issuer and their ability to tax citizens. This is an unsecured debt. Citizens generally do not enjoy paying more in taxes, which is why the municipality must balance the amount of debt they take on with what they are able to repay. This is where the debt coverage ratio comes into play, as well as the bond counsel. There are many taxes that a municipality can increase in order to cover debt expenses, such as property taxes and other ad valorem taxes. GO bonds can be contrasted with revenue bonds.

REVENUE BONDS

Revenue bonds are another form of municipal bond that are backed by user fees of some kind. Examples include fees from tolls, hospitals, higher education, leasing, transportation, water, sewer, electric, etc. Revenue bonds make up about two-thirds of the municipal bonds market, with GO

bonds roughly accounting for the other third. Something important to note with revenue bonds is that they can have two types of pledges: net or gross. A net pledge is where the issuer pledges to make payments on debts with the net income left over after operating expenses have been deducted. This is contrasted with a gross pledge, where the gross revenues are used to pay the debt. A gross pledge is a better deal for the investor as they have a higher claim on revenues from the project and are more likely to get their money than under a net pledge. Depending on the type of revenue bond, it can carry more risk. It is important to analyze the underlying project that the revenue bond is backed by in order to ascertain the risk inherent to the bond and if the yield justifies the risk.

OTHER TYPES OF MUNICIPAL SECURITIES

A special tax municipal bond can be thought of as a blend between a GO bond and a revenue bond. Just as the name suggests, they are backed by a specific tax. These specific taxes could be taxes on cigarettes, a casino, property, etc. This is like a GO bond in that the payment comes from a tax source, but like a revenue bond in that it is one specific tax that covers the bond, rather than the broader taxes of the municipality. Special assessment bonds are a subset of special tax bonds and are paid by fees which are levied on specific homeowners who receive benefits from the project. For example, if the municipality were to install new streetlamps in your neighborhood, they could levy a tax on the homeowners to pay for it. This would be a special assessment.

Moral obligation bonds are a unique type of municipal debt instrument. Essentially, a moral obligation bond says that the issuer has a moral obligation to avoid defaulting on the debt, even if they must retrieve funds from elsewhere. An example of this could be a state government stepping in the fulfill the debt obligations of a municipality that cannot meet their own obligations. It is important to note that the obligation is moral and not ethical. The investor could still lose their money in the event of default and have no legal recourse against the issuer.

The attractiveness of municipal securities comes in the form of their advantageous tax treatment. Qualified municipal bonds are exempt from federal income tax and can be exempt from state and local income tax as well (if the investor resides in the state of the issued bond). This applies to interest on the bond—if an investor were to buy a bond for a discount in the secondary market and hold it to maturity without accreting the cost basis, they would be subject to taxes on their capital gains. "Munies" are particularly attractive to investors in higher income tax brackets, as they provide a form of partially-tax free income.

Double-barreled municipal bonds are a special type of bond where the interest and principal payments are backed by both the revenue of the distinct project and the taxing authority of the issuer. As you can see, this is essentially a merger of the GO and revenue bonds, yet different from special tax bonds. This is attractive to investors as it increases the security and safety of their capital. However, these bonds usually have a lower interest rate due to the higher security. As with most things, risk and reward have a proportional relationship.

OTHER TYPES OF DEBT INSTRUMENTS

Money market instruments are high-quality debt with a maturity date of less than one year. Money market instruments include commercial paper, CDs, T-Bills, and repos. There are also money market mutual funds that investors can purchase which are made up of various money market securities. These securities are highly liquid due to their short maturity and are secure investments. They are attractive investments for investors looking for safety of principle and preservation of capital. Sometimes, investors will "park" money in money market funds while they wait for the economy to shift or for a good opportunity to arise in the market.

Certificates of deposit are one of the most common types of money market funds that many investors are familiar with. They pay a fixed interest rate and have maturities that can range from a few months to many years. The maturity decides whether or not the CD would be considered a money market instrument. You can consider CDs to be a step up from savings accounts; they pay a higher interest rate but are less liquid as the money cannot be withdrawn (without penalty) until the CD matures. Most banks and credit unions offer CDs, but they can also be bought out in the market. There are also instruments referred to as negotiable jumbo CDs. They have a minimum balance of $100,000.

Bankers' acceptances are another form of money market instrument that act as time drafts that can be ordered from banks to serve as protection against counterparty risk. They are typically issued in multiples of $100,000 and have maturities that range from 90–180 days. In a way, they act as certified checks or cashiers' checks. They are common in international trade as well. They can be purchased on the secondary market, similar to zero-coupon bonds. They are issued at a discount and have a max maturity of 270 days, just like commercial paper.

Commercial paper is a common form of money market instrument that is issued by corporations as a way to get around the SEC's requirement to register long-term securities and to help finance upcoming payables. They have a max maturity of 270 days with an average of 30 days, which classifies them as short-term securities. They are also issued at a discount, like bankers' acceptances. They are essentially large-form unsecured borrowing by corporations which can lead to greater risks than other money market instruments like CDs. They also have a minimum denomination of $100,000, like bankers' acceptances and jumbo CDs. They pay a coupon in line with prevailing market interest rates.

MATURITIES

Money market instruments have maturities of one year or less and are thought of as short-term debt instruments. Corporate and municipal bonds have maturities greater than one year, ranging into the decades. T-Notes have maturities of 1-10 years, with T-Bonds making up the 10-30 year maturities. Due to the way interest rates interact with bonds, long-term bonds tend to feel the volatility of interest rate changes more acutely than short-term bonds. This is why in a rapidly changing interest rate environment investors may look to shed long-term bonds by either selling them in the secondary market or by putting them back to the issuer if possible. In a low interest rate environment, the issuers may look to call bonds back and replace them with cheaper debt. Remember, interest rates and bond prices are inversely correlated. If interest rates go up, bond prices go down, and vice versa. Investors must also be aware of the ability of inflation to eat away at bond coupon payments.

INCOME GENERATION

Investors who purchase bonds are primarily interested in income. Income comes in the form of the interest payments the bonds make to the holder. Typically, bonds will pay interest semi-annually or annually, and the income is based off the yield of the bond. Usually, bonds will pay out a smaller percentage than what an investor can gain from common stock, but bonds are usually a safer investment as well. Investors put more money in bonds the older they get as safety of principle becomes more and more important. Some bonds can also pay capital gains if they are purchased at a discount. The way this is treated by the IRS will depend on if it is a treasury, municipal, or corporate bond. Interest income is taxed at the investor's marginal income tax rate unless it is an exempt security like some municipal bonds. Investors can also gain exposure to bonds by purchase bond fund ETFs or mutual funds. Together, bonds and stock make up the foundation of the securities industry.

COUPON VALUE

The coupon on a bond is simply the stated interest rate that it will pay out. Coupon is synonymous with interest in this instance. Although there is a stated coupon, bonds have four different yields that will change based on several factors. The four yields are current yield, nominal yield, yield to maturity, and yield to call. These will be higher or lower depending on if the bond is sold at a discount or at a premium. If a bond is sold at a discount, then the current yield will be the lowest, followed by nominal yield, yield to maturity, and yield to call. The inverse is true for bonds sold at a premium. You can calculate the current yield by dividing the bond's annual coupon by the price.

PAR VALUE

The par value of a bond refers to the stated or face value of the instrument. For bonds, par value is normally $1,000. If a bond sells for less than this, it is sold at a discount. If sold above $1,000, it is a premium bond. The par value helps to calculate the interest income on a bond. If a bond has a 5% coupon, then it's annual interest income will be $50 (1000 * 0.05). If a bond pays interest semi-annually then this would be two $25 payments.

YIELD

The yield on a bond refers to the percentage return you get on your money. It is calculated by taking the annual coupon and dividing it by the bond price. As you can see, this is why yields change as the price of the bond changes. If a bond sells at a discount, then its yield will increase if the coupon stays the same; you are earning a higher percentage since it's the same coupon for a smaller amount of capital. The opposite is true for bonds sold at a premium; your yield will be smaller as you're paying more for the same percentage return. Yields on bonds such as the ten-year treasury yield factor heavily into overall sentiment for the economy. The higher bond yields are, the more attractive they appear to investors and the less attractive equities look.

RATINGS AND RATING AGENCIES

The two major rating agencies in the bond market are Standard and Poor's (S&P) and Moody's, with Fitch's making up a smaller portion of the market. For S&P, AAA is the highest rating that can be given to a bond. U.S. government securities and high-grade corporate bonds would fall into this category. The lowest investment grade rating for S&P is BBB. Anything less than BBB (BB and lower) is considered speculative grade or "junk." Investors should steer clear of junk bonds. For Moody's, the highest rating for a bond is Aaa, with Baa being the lowest for investment grade bonds. Fitch's uses the same scale as S&P. Usually, the higher a bond's rating is, the safer an investment it represents. These ratings take into account an issuer's history of paying debt, their financial strength, and other factors that affect their ability to pay back loans. Bonds with lower ratings are usually forced to offer higher yields to attract investors. This leads to some speculative grade bonds being referred to as "income" bonds. Investors will want to stay away from these debt securities as they are not investment-grade.

CALLABLE AND CONVERTIBLE FEATURES

Bonds with a call provision can be called back by the issuer. Normally, they will have a specified time and price when the issuer can call back the bond. Issuers will do this when interest rates are falling so as to call back expensive debt and reissue cheaper debt. The opposite of this would be a put provision that allows the bond holder to put the bond back on the issuer prior to maturity. Convertible bonds are similar to convertible preferred stock. They can be converted into the company's common stock at a set price and ratio. This gives convertible bonds an option to engage in capital appreciation, which is very attractive to investors. Convertible bonds pay a lower coupon than normal bonds.

SHORT-TERM VS. LONG-TERM CHARACTERISTICS

Short-term bonds mature in a few years, and long-term bonds typically mature in decades. Because of the way interest rates interact with bond yields, long-term bonds are more sensitive to interest rate changes than short-term bonds. There is something called the yield curve which graphs bond yields from one year maturities to 30 years. A normal yield curve plots short-term yields as lower than long-term yields. An inverted yield curve would see long-term yields as lower than short-term yields. A flat yield curve sees both short-term and long-term yields as roughly equal. The yield curve is a very important tool for analyzing the market and weighs heavily on investor sentiment.

RELATIONSHIP BETWEEN PRICE AND INTEREST RATE

Bond prices have an inverse relationship to interest rates. When the Fed raises rates, then bond prices will start to fall, and vice versa. This is because as interest rates go up the cost of capital increases as it is more expensive to borrow money. The more expensive it is to borrow, the less likely issuers are to authorize more debt in the form of bonds. When interest rates are low, such as in a period of low inflation and economic growth, then bonds are an attractive investment. Additionally, when inflation soars and market sentiment turns bearish, investors flock from riskier equities to safer bonds and money market securities. Remember, bond prices and interest rates are inversely correlated.

NEGOTIATED VS. COMPETITIVE OFFERINGS VIA UNDERWRITERS AND SYNDICATES

Just like with stocks, issuers of debt will use underwriters to help sell the bonds to the public. This can take one of two forms: negotiated, or competitive. A negotiated underwriting is where the issuer will select an underwriter first without any bidding or competition. Contrast this with competitive underwriting, where various underwriters bid for the issuer's business and the issuer chooses the best deal with the lowest interest cost among the pool of options. Competitive underwriting tends to be more popular, especially for municipalities, as it usually results in less cost to the issuer. There are various other factors that go into how a bond is organized with an underwriter, such as credit ratings, the size of the issue, whether it is a new issue, etc.

AUCTION

Treasury securities are sold at auction. Trillions of dollars' worth of Treasury securities are sold this way hundreds of times a year. Investors can buy securities directly from the auction or purchase them through their broker. There is also an active secondary market for Treasury securities, which means an investor can purchase from auction, and then sell to the market. T-Bonds, T-Notes, T-Bills, Floating Rate Notes (FRNs), and TIPS are all sold at auction. These auctions determine the yield, rate, and/or discount margin of these securities based off prevailing market demand as well as interest rates.

OPTIONS
TYPES OF OPTIONS
PUTS AND CALLS

Stock options are a financial derivative, meaning they derive their value from an underlying asset. In the case of stock options, they derive their value from the underlying common stock of the company. Options can be confusing, but at their most basic level they are simply a way for an investor to speculate on the movement of a stock either upwards or downwards. A call option speculates that a share's price will increase, whereas a put option speculates that it will decrease. These are different than going long or short on stock. When you go long on stock you purchase shares at the market price. Think of shorting as a way to speculate that the share price will go down. A short seller borrows shares (usually from their broker), then sells them in the market, hoping to buyback the position at a later time (hopefully when the share price is lower) thus making a gain on the spread. Short selling is inherently riskier thanks to something called unlimited risk. You can also go long or short on options. Since options are leveraged, they are riskier than simply buying the stock outright, therefore they are not suitable for all investors.

EQUITY VS. INDEX

Equity options are stock options for listed common stock of a company. If you buy calls on IBM, Microsoft, or Apple, you are buying equity options. An index option is a stock option on an index such as the DJIA, S&P 500, or NASDAQ. There are specific types of index options that follow the index, and there are also index options for ETFs that track those indexes. SPDRs are a popular index option, with the SPY S&P 500 ETF being one of the most actively traded ETFs in the world. There are also leveraged ETFs that return 2x or 3x of the underlying ETF. There are also inverse versions of these ETFs. For example, if you buy a 3x leveraged inverse SPY ETF and SPY goes up by 1%, your ETF will go down by 3%. You can also buy options on these leveraged ETFs, which can lead to extremely leveraged positions.

HEDGING AND SPECULATION

Investors can hedge their stock positions through the use of options in several ways. If an investor owns 100 shares of Apple and they want to protect themselves against downside risk, they can buy a put option on Apple. If Apple goes down, the shares decrease in value while the put increases in value. The reverse of this is true if they are short a stock. If you have 100 shares of Apple short, you can buy a call to protect yourself against the unlimited loss potential of short positions. Options can also be used as a hedge against other options through many strategies, such as straddles and spreads. Large funds routinely hold put options against their long stock or call options against their short stock to hedge their positions. Individual investors can take advantage of this strategy as well.

EXPIRATION DATES

Traditionally, options expire on the third Friday of the month at 11:59PM ET. However, there are many option chains that have expirations ranging from weekly to every couple of days, as is the case with SPY. The further an option is from expiration, the more expensive it is. This is due to time value. The option has a greater chance of being in the money the further you are from expiration. Theta measures the time decay of an option and gets progressively more aggressive as you move within 45 to 30 days of expiration. This is similar to how warrants operate. The longer you have until maturity, the greater your chance of being able to exercise your position.

STRIKE PRICE

The strike price of a stock refers to the point at which the option is in the money. If a stock is trading at 10.00 and your option's strike is 11.00, then your option is in the money once the stock price passes 11.00. At the money would be if the stock was exactly at 11.00 and out of the money would be anything below 11.00. The further a strike is from the current share price, the less expensive the contract. This is because the chance of an option going in the money gets increasingly less likely as you move further from the share price. Options that are in the money already are more expensive than options that are out of the money for the same reason. Just because you hold an in the money option does not mean you must exercise it. You can always sell the option back to the market and walk away with a profit if the value of the option is higher than what you initially bought it at.

PREMIUMS

The premium of an option is the amount that the buyer pays to the seller for the right to hold that option. Remember that an option is a derivative and derives its value from the underlying security. An option gives the holder of the contract the ability to exercise the option when in the money and receive 100 shares of the underlying at the strike price. Premiums get more expensive the more volatile an option is as well as the further it is from expiration. The Greeks are the factors that influence the premium price of options, but they are not essential to know for the SIE. Remember that the seller, the one who writes the option, receives the premium as payment for taking on risk, whereas the buyer and holder of the option pays the premium for the right to exercise the option when in the money.

SETTLEMENT TYPES

Stock options can normally settle one of two ways: underlying or cash. When an equity stock option is held to expiration and is in the money, the holder can exercise the option, which means they will receive 100 shares of the underlying stock at the strike price from the writer of the option. With index options, they can only be settled for cash. This means if you hold call options on SPY and hold till expiration with the contract in the money, you will receive cash rather than shares of SPY. Now, the holder of the option is not required to hold the option till expiration and exercise. Instead, an investor can trade options before expiration in an attempt to make a profit off the difference in premiums paid. If you buy an option for $500, and the value increases to $600, you can make a $100 profit off the difference between what you paid and what you sold for. This is not very different from trading stocks.

IN-THE-MONEY OR OUT-OF-THE MONEY

Options are categorized as either in the money or out of the money. An in the money option is where the market price of the underlying security is above the strike price of the contract (for a call option—put options would need the market price to be below the strike in order to be in the money). Out of money options would be the opposite. If you have a call option with a strike of $50 while the underlying is at $45, you are out of the money. If the underlying appreciates $51, you are now in the money. ITM options can be exercised immediately if they're American style. Intrinsic value refers to the value the option would have if exercised at that moment. ITM options obviously have greater intrinsic value than OTM options.

COVERED VS. UNCOVERED OPTIONS

When selling (writing) an option, there are two ways to go about it. The first is the conservative way, which requires the seller to cover their position through either securities or cash. A covered call is when an investor sells a call against stock they already own. If the option is exercised, their shares will be called away. Think of it like a secured loan. On the put side, the option can be secured

41

by cash held in the investor's account. Uncovered or "naked" options are inherently riskier. This involves selling options against stock you do not own. This is accomplished through margin, the borrowing of shares, or the use of surrogate options to replace the use of shares. Understand that uncovered positions are riskier than covered positions, since naked positions are subject to unlimited risk, similar to short selling.

AMERICAN VS. EUROPEAN OPTIONS

There are two main styles of options: American and European. The difference is in the investor's ability to exercise an option. With American options, the investor can exercise at any time as long as the contract is in the money. This is usually the case with equity options. With European contracts, the investor can only exercise at expiration. This is usually associated with non-equity options. Most options you run into on stocks are going to be of the American style.

EXERCISE AND ASSIGNMENT

When an option is exercised by the holder, we say that the writer of the option is assigned. This means they must meet the assignment by providing either shares or cash, depending on the contract. Now, assignment is not always a bad thing. In the case with covered calls, investors will usually sell calls with a strike above the market price of the shares they own. If the shares appreciate to the strike price and are exercised, then the investor receives capital gains from the stock on top of the premium earned from the option. This can also effectively cap a person's gains. If you have hold stock at $45 and have to sell at $50, but the stock goes all the way to $60, you've essentially missed out on $1000 worth of gains. A similar concept applies to the use of put options.

STRATEGIES FOR OPTIONS

Buying an option equates to going long on that position, while selling the option equals going short. Long calls are betting the stock will go up, short calls are expecting the stock to remain roughly neutral. Long puts are expecting the stock to decline, and short puts are expecting the stock to remain neutral or appreciate. Many investors will use combinations of options to hedge different positions. If you're long on stock, then holding a few long puts can be good downside protection. If you're short stock, then long calls can fill the same role. Understanding the relationship between different options can help investors to be more sophisticated in their positions and portfolios.

When you start to combine multiple option contracts into one portfolio, you begin to create more complex positions. A spread is when an investor buys two options and either puts both or calls both. When you buy one option with a lower strike and sell an option with a higher strike, that is a credit spread. The flip of this would be a debit spread. A straddle would be buying two different types of contracts, one call and one put. You buy at the same strike and expiration for both and only make money when one of the contracts exceeds the breakeven point (which you get from adding the premiums paid) from the strike price. You can mix and match these positions and create butterflies, iron condors, horizontal and vertical spreads, and a slew of other positions with different characteristics and advantages.

SPECIAL DISCLOSURES

The Options Disclosure Document is a piece of paperwork that must accompany certain options sales literature and advertising. This helps to inform the potential investor of the risks associated with options. When an investor opens up an option account, they must sign and return the options agreement within 15 days of account approval or have their account restricted. It is essential to remember that the ODD must accompany options advertising like worksheets and similar documents.

OPTIONS CLEARING CORPORATION (OCC) FOR LISTED OPTIONS

The Options Clearing Corporation is the issuer and guarantor of all options contracts. This eliminates counter-party risk for options investors. This means if you try to exercise a call option and the writer is unable to deliver, the OCC will step in and make good on the contract. This helps to stabilize the market and alleviate investor fears. This plays a similar role to the FDIC or SIPC in that the OCC essentially ensures the holder of an option against the risk of counterparties failing to deliver on promises. It is important not to confuse the OCC with the Chicago Board of Options Exchange, which is an options exchange and SRO.

PACKAGED PRODUCTS
INVESTMENT COMPANIES

Investment companies fall under three broad categories: management companies, unit investment companies, and face amount certificate companies. Face amount certificate companies no longer exist in the United States. Unit investment companies can be subdivided into fixed and non-fixed UITs. The same goes for management companies, which can be subdivided into closed-end funds (publicly traded funds) and open-end funds (mutual funds). These are largely regulated by the Investment Company Act of 1940.

CLOSED-END FUNDS

Closed-end management companies, also known as publicly traded funds, are a form of management company. These companies issue a fixed number of shares at an initial public offering that they use to fund their investment activities. These shares then trade on the secondary market. An example of a closed-end fund would be a municipal bond fund. The prices of these funds can change as supply and demand affects the market. We would say that closed-end fund shares are negotiable rather than redeemable, since they are traded on an exchange similar to common stock.

OPEN-END FUNDS

An open-end fund is the traditional mutual fund that people talk about. They are actively managed and charge a management fee usually based off the assets under management (AUM) of the fund. They normally have a defined investment objective, such as growth funds, bond funds, money market funds, etc. They do not trade on an exchange and instead are purchased directly from the mutual fund company. They are redeemable, meaning that shares must be redeemed with the issuer rather than sold to another investor. They can have sales charges, contingent deferred sales charges, and 12b-1 fees, which are marketing fees. There are Class A, B, and C shares that have different fee structures and time horizons that they are suited for. Mutual funds can be a costly investment as many funds can struggle to "beat the market" while also charging investors many fees. The advent of the Exchange-Traded Fund siphoned demand away from mutual funds and towards low-cost ETFs.

UNIT INVESTMENT TRUSTS (UITS)

When someone refers to a UIT, they are talking about an investment company that is similar to both a closed-end fund and an open-end fund. UITs are similar to mutual funds, as they buy up a collection of stocks and bonds and then sell units of this portfolio to investors at a specified price. They can be sold via IPO and sometimes traded on a secondary market but usually are redeemed with the issuer. They are passively managed. A fixed UIT does not make changes to the underlying portfolio. A non-fixed UIT can make changes to the portfolio.

VARIABLE CONTRACTS/ANNUITIES

A variable annuity is a type of fixed-income investment that serve as a retirement vehicle. They are non-qualified (meaning they do not allow contributions to serve as tax-deductible events) and are basically a mutual fund with an insurance label. Investors can begin distributions at 59 ½ and must distribute by 72. They follow a Last-In First-Out accounting method for determining costs basis, which means that the last units purchased are the first ones sold for means of determining taxes. These are attractive investments for people close to retirement as income and safety are normally priorities for retirement.

44

Mometrix

LOADS

A no-load fund means that the management company does not charge a sales charge on transactions to purchase shares of the fund. Loads can refer to both the initial sales charge or commissions charged to the customer. Different share classes are designated as either load or no-load funds. Some shares have something called a contingent deferred sales charge that is not charged until the investor actually sells the shares and can sometimes go to zero if held for long enough by the investor. No-load funds are normally more attractive to investors, as fees can eat away at any alpha (investment return above a benchmark) generated by the fund. It's important to note that no-load funds can never charge more than 0.75 points, and any 12b-1 promotional fees must be no more than 0.25 points.

SHARE CLASSES

There are usually three main share classes when it comes to mutual funds: Class A shares, Class B shares, and Class C shares. Class A shares typically charge an up-front sales charge and have lower 12b-1 fees than the other share classes. They are typically more attractive for long-term investors. Class B shares have high exit fees and greater expense ratios. They can sometimes be converted into Class A shares. Class B shares are usually not the answer for investors, at least in test world. Class C shares are characterized by a higher sales fee than a Class A share and an exit fee that is sometimes waived. There are also breakpoints that have to be factored into calculations for the sales charge on these share classes.

NET ASSET VALUE (NAV)

The NAV is a calculation that mutual funds use to determine the value of their fund. The NAV is calculated at the end of every day. NAV is not priced intra-day. NAV is calculated by taking assets and subtracting out liabilities. Investors will usually pay the Public Offering Price (POP) when purchasing mutual fund shares. Depending on the type of fund, the investor may be paying the POP or the NAV, depending on if it is bought in the secondary market or directly from the issuer.

DISCLOSURES

Mutual funds must disclose any and all fees to potential investors via a prospectus. This includes any sales charges, 12b-1 fees, and the expense ratio of the fund. Remember that mutual funds are a relatively expensive investment vehicle due to the active professional management of the fund. This is contrasted with cheaper, passive options like ETFs, or even UITs to an extent. It is also important to note that since mutual funds have various share classes, it is important to make sure investors are aware of the fees associated with each share class.

COSTS AND FEES

Mutual funds are notorious for charging high fees, especially since the creation of the ETF with expense ratios as low as 0.05%. Most mutual funds will charge a sales charge on initial transactions. This can be reduced by following the breakpoint schedule or through the use of a LOI. There are also 12b-1 fees charged on the front end of the fund (depending on the type of fund), as well as surrender charges. There's also the general fee charged to investors for simply being in the fund. This is a function of assets under management as well as fund performance. In the eyes of mutual fund managers, you get what you pay for. The hope is that you will recoup your money lost to costs and fees in the form of superior fund performance compared to the market, but this is not always the case. Understanding the fee structure associated with various mutual funds is essential for determining suitability with an investor.

45

BREAKPOINTS

Mutual funds that are load funds will normally charge a different sales fee depending on the size of the purchase. For instance, the sales charge for a $25,000 purchase may be 6%, whereas the sales charge for a $100,000 purchase may be 2%. These breakpoints are established at certain intervals where, if reached, the sales charge for the entire transaction is reduced. Something that is very important to remember is that RRs cannot sell mutual funds to investors without making them aware of the breakpoint schedule or selling them mutual fund amounts directly under the breakpoint. This is known as a breakpoint sale and is prohibited by FINRA.

RIGHT OF ACCUMULATION (ROA)

If an investor does not have the funds to hit a certain breakpoint for a mutual fund, they can still receive it later. Mutual funds offer right of accumulation, which basically means that when a customer purchases additional units of the fund they will be added to the cost basis of the existing position. This means if there is a breakpoint at $15,000, and the investor currently has $13,000, they can purchase $2,000 more to secure the breakpoint and discounted sales charge. This is advantageous for investors as they do not have to worry so much about making lump sum investments; they can build a position overtime and still secure breakpoint discounts.

LETTER OF INTENT (LOI)

A letter of intent is a document an investor can send to a mutual fund promising to purchase more units at a later date in order to secure a discounted sales charge right now. This allows an investor to secure a breakpoint now even though they do not have the funds to secure it currently. The letter of intent is normally good for a period of 13 months. It can also be backdated by 90 days. This is another tool in the investor's toolbox that can help to secure discounted sales charges and ultimately invest more money.

SURRENDER CHARGES

Simply put, a surrender charge is a fee charged to an investor for withdrawing money from an insurance contract, variable annuity, or mutual fund within a surrender period. This incentivizes investors to keep their money in the account for a longer period of time. This is one of the factors that makes annuities and mutual funds less liquid than other investment vehicles such as money market instruments. The surrender charge can vary in amount as well as time in force, but it generally covers a period of several years. This is why it can be unwise to invest money that you may need in the short-term, as you could find yourself owing a few dollars just for withdrawing your money.

SALES CHARGES

Sales charges can be a big downside to investing in mutual funds. After paying sales charges and various other fees, investors can find it difficult to actually "beat the market", which is normally the entire point of actively managed funds that attempt to generate alpha (points exceeding a benchmark such as the S&P 500). According to regulations, the maximum sales charge permitted is 8.5%. The sales charge will normally vary depending on the type of mutual fund share class, such as Class A or C. There are also 12b-1 marketing fees that can be assessed on investors and will also vary depending on share class.

MUNICIPAL FUND SECURITIES

529 PLANS

A 529 plan is a form of state-sponsored municipal fund security. Similar to UGMA and UTMA accounts, the purpose is for custodians or parents to put aside money for their children or dependents. In the case of the 529 plan, the investment objective is explicitly to fund college education, though some funds will allow a certain dollar amount to be spent on secondary education below the undergraduate level. In contrast to a Coverdell ESA, there is no income limit on contributions to a 529 plan, but any annual contribution in excess of the gift tax exclusion limit ($17,000 in 2023) is taxed as a gift. Contributions are not tax deductible, but they are exempt from federal income tax upon disbursement as long as the funds are used to pay for qualifying expenses.

A prepaid tuition 529 plan is only offered in select states and differs from a savings 529 plan since the prepaid account "locks in" current in-state tuition rates for the beneficiary of the account. This can be beneficial since university costs are constantly rising. However, prepaid accounts are limited in where and how they can be used and do not offer easy transferability to out-of-state universities. In contrast, a traditional savings 529 plan is much more versatile. Enrollment periods are more flexible for savings plans as well. However, a savings plan can have more investment risk if it is invested in riskier securities. Ultimately, whether to use a prepaid or savings 529 plan comes down to suitability and the individual investor's situation.

LOCAL GOVERNMENT INVESTMENT POOLS (LGIPS)

A local government investment pool is essentially a money market fund for local governments. It is a municipal security similar to 529 plans and ABLE accounts. Since these LGIPs are government controlled, they are exempt from SEC registration. This can be beneficial in that it allows for greater flexibility, but can be detrimental in the form of reduced insurance against loss. It is important to note that LGIPs can vary in investment objective, risk, and ratings. An investor must do their due diligence when considering investing in an LGIP.

ABLE ACCOUNTS

An ABLE account is a municipal fund investment account that exists to pay for medical expenses related to disabilities. This account is also known as a 529A account. Distributions are tax-free so long as they are used for qualified medical expenses. There are also special rollover abilities between the ABLE account and tuition 529 plans. ABLE accounts are only allowed to be used for a beneficiary with a qualified disability. It is important to check with the state to see what qualifies and what does not.

OWNER VS. BENEFICIARY

An owner of an account is typically the person who sets it up. The beneficiary is the person the account is set up for. In the case of 529 plans and ABLE accounts, the owner is typically a parent, while the beneficiary is a child, though this is not always the case. Sometimes a grandparent or other relative can set up an account for one of their relatives. It is important to understand how cost basis and sales proceeds change based on the type of account, the age of the beneficiary, when the account must transfer to the beneficiary, etc.

RESTRICTIONS ON USE OF PLAN ASSETS

Restrictions on assets generally means that specific assets can only be used for specific purposes. For example, municipal bonds can only be used for their stated purpose. In the case of municipal fund securities such as 529 plans or ABLE accounts, plan assets are restricted in their use. 529 plans can only be used to pay for qualified educational expenses. In the case of ABLE accounts, those funds can only be used to pay for qualified medical expenses. Similar restrictions apply to the

use of retirement accounts and even annuities. It is important to make sure an investor understands these restrictions before putting money into an investment vehicle.

TAX ADVANTAGES

One of the main attractions to municipal fund securities is their tax treatment. Qualified accounts used for qualified expenses can benefit from preferential tax treatment compared to other funds or accounts. For example, 529 plan distributions are tax-free as long as the funds are used for qualified educational expenses. The same goes for ABLE accounts and qualified medical expenses. Also remember that contributions to 529s are considered gifts for tax purposes, which can be more attractive than being taxed at ordinary income tax rates. ABLE account contributions can also yield a tax deduction depending on the state. Remember, since these are municipal fund securities, they will vary from state to state. This is why brokers and RRs are required to be registered in each state they do business.

DIRECT OR ADVISER SOLD

Direct-sold plans are bought directly from the issuer or sponsor such as the state in the case of 529 plans, ABLE accounts, and LGIPs. Many of these same accounts can also be advisor-sold. This means the individual opens up the account through a financial advisor or broker-dealer rather than through the state. Which method to use depends on the investor and any potential benefits that different states may offer. It is important to do one's due diligence on the difference between these two styles in your respective state.

DIRECT PARTICIPATION PROGRAMS (DPPS)

TYPES OF DPPS

LIMITED PARTNERSHIPS

Direct participation programs are a form of pooled investment that offer investors the opportunity to take advantage of the gains of a business, usually in the areas of energy such as oil. When structured as a limited partnership, there are two categories of people: the general partner and the limited partner. The limited partners provide the capital while the general partner oversees the operations of the business. Limited partners are usually only liable for their equity and cannot lose more than they put in. The general partner can be held liable for debts of the partnership. A similar structure is followed with Real Estate Investment Trusts.

TENANTS IN COMMON (TIC)

Tenants in common generally refers to either REITs or joint accounts such as partnerships. TIC means that two or more parties share ownership interest of a piece of land or an account. This can be an equal or divided interest, such as 50/50 , 60/40, etc. When one party dies, their share goes to the other party. This is a form of legal arrangement that can also be used in accounts for married couples filing jointly. This is important to understand when it comes to events such as divorce or death. This is contrasted with joint tenancy and tenancy by entirety. There are also joint tenants with rights of survivorship that can be used for joint accounts.

PASS-THROUGH TAX TREATMENT

One of the big advantages of a partnership is the use of pass-through tax treatment. A similar tax structure is adopted by sole-proprietorships, LLCs, and s-corporations under Subchapter M. Pass-through status means that losses and gains flow through the partnership to the investors. This means that gains are reported on the limited partners individual tax returns. Typically, LPs cannot get out of a partnership without the permission of the GP. They are less liquid than investing in equities or debt securities as an individual. This is a different structure for flow-through of profits as compared to corporations where income is taxed at the corporate level, then distributed in the form of dividends to investors, which is taxed at the individual level. This is concept known as "double taxation" and is one of the factors that makes partnerships an attractive investment for tax purposes.

LISTING STATUS

An investor cannot go to their brokerage and purchase shares in a partnership or DPP through the secondary market like you would shares of a company. Partnerships and DPPs are unlisted securities, meaning they do not have a prospectus that they file with the SEC similar to hedge funds and other investment vehicles. DPPs are usually only offered to accredited investors due to the illiquid nature and high risk of the investment. These are usually not suitable for retail investors who do not meet the definition of an accredited investor.

LIQUIDITY

DPPs, being unregistered securities, are inherently less liquid and thus riskier than registered securities traded on the secondary market. Limited partners must meet income and net worth thresholds for most DPPs just to put money in. Once they are invested, they are only able to withdraw funds with the permission of the general partner. This is similar to hedge funds, where the manager can hold on to the investor's funds if they so choose. Investors must be aware of the illiquidity of such investment before considering adding them to their portfolio.

REAL ESTATE INVESTMENT TRUSTS (REITS)

TYPES OF REITS

A real estate investment trust (REIT) is a type of partnership that invests in real estate. REITs can be either private, registered/non-listed, or listed (for the purposes of the SIE). REITs will typically either invest in cash-flowing properties such as office buildings, apartment complexes, and shopping malls (known as equity REITs), or will invest in the mortgages and MBS backing properties and buildings (known as mortgage REITs). REITs will vary in their tax treatment depending on the type. REITs are important for the economy as they help to add liquidity to the real estate market and stimulate the growth of development.

PRIVATE

A private REIT is simply a real estate investment trust that does not trade on an exchange, nor does it register with the SEC. Due to this setup, private REITs are normally only sold to qualified institutional buyers. Remember that Reg D and Rule 144A govern the use and sale of unregistered securities. These REITs are typically professionally managed and have various fees and costs associated with them. It is important to check the fee structure prior to investing in one of these REITs. These private REITs are also illiquid similar to DPPs.

REGISTERED, NON-LISTED

A registered, non-listed REIT is exactly what it sounds like. It is a REIT that is registered with the SEC but does not trade on any major exchanges. These can also be referred to as public, non-listed REITs or (PNLRs). These REITs must make filings with the SEC, such as quarterly and annual financial statements, that are available to the public. They can offer more liquidity than a private REIT but are still relatively illiquid. There is usually a minimum holding period that must be reached before an investor can redeem shares and withdraw funds from the REIT.

LISTED

A listed REIT is a Real Estate Investment Trust that is both registered with the SEC and listed on a public exchange. It is very testable to remember that a publicly listed REIT must invest at least 75% of total assets into real estate, cash, or U.S. Treasuries; and they must payout a minimum of 90% of taxable income to shareholders via dividends. There are various other requirements for qualification as a REIT, but those are the most testable. REITs are very liquid compared to the other form of REITs. They can be bought and sold on the secondary market at will.

REAL ESTATE EQUITY OR DEBT

Broadly, equity real estate involves investing in projects that will deliver income in the form of tenant rents and/or capital gains from the flipping and selling of property. Debt real estate would involve the issuing of loans or investing mortgages through the use of mortgage-backed securities (MBS). REITs may specialize in one of these forms of real estate investing depending on their investment objective. Investors will want to weigh the pros and cons of the two forms of real estate investment when investing in REITs.

TAX-ADVANTAGED INCOME WITHOUT DOUBLE TAXATION

Remember that double taxation is when a corporation is taxed on earnings and its distributions are taxed at the investor's ordinary income tax rate. Also remember that REITs must distribute at least 90% of their taxable income to shareholders. Due to this, REITs are not normally taxed at the trust level. If they are, it would be at corporate tax rates. Now, taxation at the investor level depends on the type of REIT and the income distributed in the form of dividends. Interest income will be taxed as ordinary income, whereas capital gains passed through to the investor will be taxed as capital gains. This will all be reported on the investor's 1099-DIV form.

HEDGE FUNDS

A hedge fund is a type of limited partnership similar to a mutual fund but only suitable for very wealthy investors. The goal is to generate alpha above a benchmark such as the S&P 500. They are extremely illiquid, and it can be years before an investor is able to redeem shares with the fund. There are also funds of hedge funds that can be thought of as a mutual fund full of different hedge funds. Hedge funds use advanced strategies in order to generate a higher return.

MINIMUM INVESTMENT REQUIREMENT

Hedge funds are only suitable for very high net worth investors. This means that investors will need to be accredited according to the SEC's definition. The fees are higher as well as the risks, so investors need to be able to tolerate significant losses without being put in a financially precarious position. Hedge funds will usually require a high initial investment, sometimes in the millions of dollars. When it comes to suitability, these are only suitable for investors with a high net worth and a high-risk tolerance.

PARTNERSHIP STRUCTURE

Hedge funds are organized as limited partnerships for tax reasons and management purposes. The investment manager serves as manager of the firm and will usually invest a significant amount of personal capital in the fund to help align interests and incentives. Another entity will serve as the general partner, similar to REITs or DPPs. The GP manages the operations of the fund. The investors are the limited partners of the fund, meaning they provide the capital and take on limited risk. There are also auditors, prime brokers, and other people involved in the structure of a hedge fund.

PRIVATE EQUITY FIRMS

A private equity firm is a business that seeks to take a controlling interest in companies and essentially flip them for a profit (though it can be more complicated than that simplification). PE firms are some of the most prestigious in the finance world and for good reason: they control large amounts of capital and are known for taking part in massive deals. As is the case with hedge funds, PE firms are typically only open to accredited and institutional investors. They carry many of the same risks that hedge funds do, such as liquidity and market risk. Where a hedge fund is focused on trading in the securities market, a PE firm's goal is to buy companies and sell them for more than they bought them for at a later date.

ILLIQUID NATURE

Since a hedge fund is only open to accredited investors, they can "get away" with a lot more than a mutual fund. One of the tools that a hedge fund has is the ability to lock up investor capital in order to survive rough times in the market and/or deal with other liquidity or capital concerns. This means an investor may not have access to their funds for years at a time. An investor in a hedge fund is considered a limited partner and cannot simply sell his shares to another investor. Remember, hedge fund shares are only redeemable with the issuer. These liquidity concerns are one of the reasons that hedge funds are only open to accredited investors who can, generally, afford to lock up millions without going bankrupt.

EXCHANGE-TRADED PRODUCTS (ETPS)

Prior to the creation of exchange-traded products, an average investor was faced with either managing their own investments or saddling up with a high-cost mutual fund. Exchange-traded products changed the industry. The two main types are exchange-traded funds (ETFs) and exchange-traded notes (ETNs). They have much lower expense ratios, are very liquid, and are both marginable in most cases. They can cover different sectors or types of bonds and give any investor access to broad diversification, effectively eliminating non-systematic risk.

TYPES OF ETPS
EXCHANGE-TRADED FUNDS (ETFS)

An ETF can be thought of as a basket of stocks that an investor can purchase shares of. They come in all different shapes and sizes. They can follow an index such as the S&P 500 or the NASDAQ; a specific market such as domestic or international; a sector within the market like tech or energy; and even types of stocks, such as dividend, growth, etc. The attractiveness of ETFs comes not only from their variety but also from the low expense ratios. Most ETFs are going to have expense ratios that range from 0.05% to 0.50%, depending on the fund. They are bought and sold on the secondary market and can be purchased with margin. There are also inverse and leveraged ETFs that can multiply both returns and risk. ETFs are passively managed, compared to mutual funds and hedge funds which are actively managed. The ETF seeks to match the performance of a benchmark, such as the S&P 500. ETFs are a very attractive asset for most investors.

EXCHANGE-TRADED NOTES (ETNS)

An ETN is similar to an ETF except that it holds debt securities rather than equities. They are a form of unsecured debt instrument and do not make periodic payments in the same way as traditional bonds. ETNs have varying maturities and will normally pay at the maturity based off the price of the index or benchmark they track. They can be sponsored by investment companies and banks. They are a good option for investors who want to diversify their debt holdings.

ALTERNATIVE INVESTMENTS TO MUTUAL FUNDS

Mutual funds are notorious for high fees, limited investor power, and illiquidity. Exchange-traded products help to serve as an alternative to the once mighty mutual fund. ETFs and ETNs are low-cost, flexible, can track many different sectors and industries, and are very liquid. When these products were first introduced, they greatly disrupted the financial industry and for good reason. There is a growing trend towards lower and lower fees in the financial industry, with most large brokerages now effecting zero commission trades for customers. This is good news for investors, who will be able to keep more of their money invested rather than paying for the opportunity to invest. It also gives retail investors greater bargaining power and the ability to affect the market and its movements.

FEE CONSIDERATIONS

Although ETFs and ETNs are considered to be low-cost, they are not zero-cost. ETFs will have an expense ratio that is charged to the investor that will normally be a fraction of a percent. For an ETN, the fees are usually imposed once maturity is reached and subtracted out from any capital appreciation. This is still advantageous compared to mutual funds, as the fees are much lower and less complicated than traditional mutual fund fee structure. Some hedge funds can charge fees as high as a 2% management fee and a 20% fee on profits, which is astronomical when compared with ETFs.

ACTIVE MANAGEMENT

A mutual fund is actively managed. This means the investment manager seeks to generate a return (alpha) in excess of the performance of a benchmark, normally the S&P 500 Index. The hope is that professional management of a fund will allow investors to generate superior returns, even after costly fees, though this is not always the case. Contrast this with a passively managed fund like an ETF. These instruments seek to match the performance of a benchmark rather than exceed it. An S&P 500 Index Fund, for example, will purchase securities in proportion to their representation in the S&P 500. This means that the ETF should closely follow the index. Given the low fees associated with ETFs, they can end up generating superior returns to mutual funds after fees are taken out.

Investment Risks

DEFINITION AND IDENTIFICATION OF RISK TYPES

Reward without risk is a happy ideal that sadly does not exist. In a market driven by supply and demand, as well as investor confidence, earnings expectations, and macroeconomic cycles, there are many things that can affect the price of a stock, bond, or alternative investment. Risks come in many forms depending on the investment vehicle. Depending on the investor, an investor may be tolerant towards certain risks but intolerant to others. For instance, a young investor is probably more risk tolerant than an investor nearing retirement. Understanding risk and its relationship to reward and the investor is essential for understanding suitability and how people interact with investing.

CAPITAL

Capital risk is probably the simplest one to understand. Capital risk is the risk of losing the money you put into your investment. Assets with a higher capital risk carry a higher chance that you will lose your money. Now this doesn't necessarily mean your investment will go to zero, just that you may lose some of your principle. Investments like stocks are going to carry more capital risk than Treasury Bonds, for instance. Generally, investments with higher capital risk should also carry higher growth potential, either in the form of income or capital appreciation. An example of this is a growth stock that varies in price regularly but overall can deliver a superior return to "safer" investments.

CREDIT

Credit risk is associated with debt instruments. Credit risk is the risk of default on a bond. This means that an issuer cannot pay its debt and you will lose either principal or interest, or both. This can happen often, especially amongst junk corporate bonds or bonds of countries that go bankrupt. Most recently, the country of Greece had a massive debt crisis where it was unable to pay off their loans and had to keep borrowing more and more money just to meet their debt service obligations. It is a slippery slope that can lead to total disaster. In some cases of default, a higher authority will step in to assume the debt. Such would be the case in a moral obligation municipal bond, where the state government may take on the debts of the municipality. Credit risk is usually measured by the rating agencies. Remember AAA or Aaa are the highest, and anything below BBB or Baa is less than investment grade.

CURRENCY

Currency risk is associated with buying securities in foreign markets. It is also referred to as exchange rate risk and it is the risk that exchange rates will fluctuate when your money is invested in foreign currencies, causing the value of those investments to depreciate. Usually, when investing in foreign securities through vehicles such as bonds, emerging markets funds, or even ADRs, there is also political risk assumed. Currency risk can be reduced by investing in highly rated countries and making sure that your money is diversified instead of being concentrated in a single currency.

INFLATIONARY/PURCHASING POWER

Inflationary risk is the risk that your money will lose value over time due to the erosion of inflation. This is especially a problem for securities where your capital is locked up for a specified period of time, such as bonds. Purchasing power risk is the risk that you will wind up with less buying power even though your capital may have appreciated. This is normally associated with bonds more than equities. Investors will want to be diversified in both common stock and fixed income securities to heal deal with inflationary risk.

INTEREST RATE/REINVESTMENT

Remember that interest rates and bonds have an inverse relationship. Interest rate risk is the risk that when your bonds mature or are called away, you will be unable to secure the same yield that you had originally. This is largely due to the fluctuation in the interest rate environment. This is especially common in MBS when prepayment risk can cause investors to scramble looking for a new investment as interest rates drop. Again, diversification is essential to keep interest rate risk from dominating a portfolio.

LIQUIDITY

Liquidity risk is simply the risk that you will not be able to easily get your money back from an investment. It doesn't necessarily mean you're losing money, just that it is locked up without you being able to access it. This is a common risk in securities such as DPPs, Private Placements, Hedge Funds, Mutual Funds, REITs, etc. Anytime you are buying a security that is not actively traded on the secondary market there is usually greater liquidity risk. In addition, stocks with large spreads or low volume have greater liquidity risk. This is common during after-hours trading or trading on penny stocks and other micro-cap companies.

MARKET/SYSTEMATIC

Market or systematic risk is the risk that the market as a whole will decline, regardless of what you are invested in. For instance, if the S&P 500 pulls back by 5%, that would be systematic risk. This is normally contrasted with non-systematic risk. A way that systematic risk is measured is usually through the form of a stock's beta coefficient. A stock with a beta of +1 is said to have systematic risk but not non-systematic risk since it moves in the same direction and speed as the rest of the market. It is important to note that systematic risk cannot be diversified away.

NON-SYSTEMATIC

Non-systematic risk, sometimes referred to as selection risk, is stock-specific risk. For instance, a tech company whose stock fluctuates greatly or has a beta greater than +1 is said to have non-systematic risk. This is because the stock moves more than the market. These companies can generate superior returns but can also experience large pullbacks. Non-systematic risk can be diversified away by investing in other sectors/companies and decreasing exposure to single stocks.

POLITICAL

Political risk is associated with investments in foreign countries. There is a threat of instability or default in countries with poor ratings or unstable governments. Investing in these companies, whether it be in the form of debt or equity, can be a risky business. Companies can be shut down and investors could lose all of their money with no recourse for getting it back. This is why due diligence must be done on any investments outside of the US, as not every government has the same rules and regulations as the United States.

PREPAYMENT

Prepayment risk is the risk that debt obligations will be paid in advance, causing the sponsor to be left without their investment. This is associated with a declining interest rate environment and reinvestment risk. If I hold a bond at 8% and it's called by the issuer since interest rates have declined and the best equivalent bond available to me now only pays 4%, that would be prepayment risk in action. Generally, CMOs and callable fixed income securities have prepayment risk, especially since the interest rate environment can be quite volatile.

STRATEGIES FOR MITIGATION OF RISK

Risk and the mitigation of risk is one of the most talked about concepts in the securities industry. If there was no risk, then everyone would be invested in securities. The unfortunate reality is that there is quite a lot of risk involved in investing. This is why there are many tools, tactics, and strategies that have been created and deployed over the years to deal with risk. This can be in the way a portfolio is constructed through strategic and tactical asset management. It could be in the way money is put into investments, such as dollar-cost-averaging, lump-sum investing, or the barbell, ladder, and bullet strategies associated with bonds. There are many ways to mitigate risk, and the exact strategies used are going to depend on the investor and their portfolio as well as the broader macroeconomic conditions at the time.

DIVERSIFICATION

Everyone has heard the saying "Don't put all your eggs in one basket." That is essentially the strategy of diversification. Remember that by diversifying our money across different investments, maturities, and issuers we can reduce or nearly eliminate non-systematic risk. Then we are just left with market risk and any other risks associated with the investments we choose, such as interest rate or political risk. The simplest way to diversify for most investors is going to be by purchasing a mutual fund or ETF that tracks the market as a whole rather than trying to pick individual stocks to outperform the market. The level of diversification needed is going to depend heavily on suitability with the customer, but some level of diversification is almost always a good thing. Not losing money is more important than making money.

PORTFOLIO REBALANCING

Portfolio rebalancing has to do with strategic and tactical asset management. Strategic asset management is deciding how much an investor wants to invest in particular securities, such as 20% in Treasuries, 40% in common stock, 40% in corporate bonds, etc. Tactical asset management is the permitted variance within each of these allocations. For instance, an investor may want 35% of their portfolio in common stock, but they are willing for it to fluctuate by 5% in either direction (30%-40%) before they feel the need to rebalance. Rebalancing is when the investor or whoever is in control of the account sells certain positions and possibly buys into others to get us back to our strategic allocations. For example, if I want only 20% of my entire portfolio in common stock, but I hold a stock that shoots up by say 50%, that is going to make my portfolio over-weighted in common stock compared to where I want to be. What we would then do is sell some of the stock and reinvest the remainder in other areas of the portfolio to get us back to the 20% target allocation. Some ETFs and mutual funds will do this on a monthly basis or more or less frequently. Failure to rebalance can lead to unnecessary non-systematic risk.

HEDGING

Hedging is an extremely popular strategy whether you are an individual investor or a hedge fund manager. At its most basic level, hedging is purchasing positions that will perform well if your other positions perform poorly. It is essentially accepting a reduction in total potential return for a minimization of risk. A common example of this would be an investor buying put contracts on the S&P 500 when they hold S&P 500 index funds. This way, if the market goes down, their puts will gain value, offsetting the unrealized loss in their long position. There are many ways to work with hedging and they get progressively more complex. Straddles, strangles, spreads and the other options strategies make great use of hedging to reduce risk in a position. You can also hedge a position through shorting or inverse ETFs, but purchasing put contracts tends to be more popular due to their comparatively cheap cost and great flexibility.

Understanding Trading, Customer Accounts, and Prohibited Activities

Trading, Settlement and Corporate Actions

ORDERS AND STRATEGIES

TYPES OF ORDERS

A market order is the most basic type of order that can be entered in a trade. When a customer places a market order, they want that order to be filled as soon as possible and at the best available price. Market orders for investors will be filled at the ask price as listed for the stock. This is the simplest type of order as there are no price qualifications or thresholds. Market orders can be dangerous if a stock is rapidly surging, as there is no limit on how much the order can be filled for. If a stock is rapidly increasing in price, a customer could end up paying much more for the stock than the original ask price listed. This is one of the reasons orders like limits are popular.

A round lot order is an order in increments of 100 (100, 200, 300, etc.). These are typical for large institutional investors (as most individual investors are not frequently purchasing tens of thousands of dollars' worth of securities at a time). An odd lot order would be anything other than a round lot purchase (23, 56, 72, etc.). This leads to the odd-lot theory, which states that small investors tend to purchase in odd lots and the small investor is always wrong. This means institutional investors will tend to trade in the opposite direction of odd lot interests. This is one of the strategies that technical analysts may employ when trying to turn a profit off of stocks.

A stop order does have a qualifying price that must be met for execution. There are two types of stop orders: buy stops and sell stops (stop loss). A sell stop is used when there is a long position that the customer wants to set a sell floor for. This means that the sell stop order will be placed at a price below the current market price of the stock. For example, if a customer is long XYZ stock at $50 and wants to protect their position, they could set a sell stop at $45. This means if XYZ declines to $45 the sell stop will trigger and sell the stock. This gives piece of mind to an investor as it allows them to quantify their downside risk (rather than the risk being the stock goes to zero). This is why sell stops are referred to as stop losses, as they set a limit on how much a position can move in a negative direction.

The other kind of stop order is the buy stop. This is used to protect a short position and is therefore placed with a price above the CMP of the stock. For example, if a customer is short ABC at $30, they could set a buy stop for $35 and it would function much the same way as a sell stop. Now, this is especially important since short positions have unlimited risk. In a long position, the worst that can happen is the stock goes to zero and you lose your entire principal amount. In a short position, since you do not own the stock you are shorting and since stock prices can theoretically move upwards ad infinitum, you are subject to unlimited risk. This is why having a buy stop order to limit that risk is so attractive to investors with a short interest.

A trailing stop order is an order to either buy or sell a security to take profit or limit loss. They can be set as a defined percentage or dollar amount away from the CMP. A trailing stop can be used to set a limit on how much the investor wants to take away from a position. If a customer buys XYZ at $50 and sets a trailing stop for 10%, then the stop order will execute and the broker will attempt to sell the position when XYZ dips to or below $45 (a 10% decrease from $50). The interesting aspect

57

of the trailing stop order is that the stop can be adjusted as the stock moves upwards. Say that XYZ moves to $75 a share—the stop trigger will be adjusted to $67.5 (10% below $75). This allows an investor to not worry about resetting a stop loss since it is automatically adjusted. This can also be used with short positions.

A limit order is an order that gives the investor the ability to choose the price they want to open or close a position with. Remember that stop orders are used to close positions, whether with a closing sale in the case of a long position, or the closing purchase in the case of a short position. The buy limit order is used when an investor wants to open a position at a certain price or better. This means that the buy limit order is going to be set below the CMP of the stock. For example, if XYZ is currently trading at $25 but the investor does not want to pay that much for it (for whatever reason), they can set a buy limit order at, for instance, $20. This means that if XYZ declines to $20 or below the buy limit order will trigger, purchasing the stock.

A sell limit order is used in a long position to set a price for the position to be closed at or better. This means that the sell limit is set above the CMP of the stock. This allows an investor to take a gain on a position. For example, XYZ is trading at $35 and a sell limit is placed at $45. If/when XYZ advances to or above $45, the order will execute and the position will be sold. This is another way for investors to have more control over their positions and their risks, as well as maximum gain.

A stop-limit order is like a hybrid between the stop and limit order types. It combines features of both order types and is suitable in situations where control is wanted over when the order should be filled. For this type of order, an investor must specify a stop point and a limit point. The stop point is the start point of the trade and is what triggers the subsequent limit order. The limit order is the price target for the trade. For instance, you could place a stop-limit order with the stop order below the CMP and the limit order below that. This is slightly more sophisticated than either order on their own but is still a good tool in the investor's toolbox.

Good-til-cancelled (GTC) orders are contrasted with day orders. A day order is exactly what it sounds like, the order is only good for that trading day and will be removed at the end of the day. A GTC order is good until cancelled by the investor. This is beneficial for limit and stop orders where the desired movement of the stock might not occur the same day that the order is placed. For most brokerages however, GTC orders will still expire after 60 days.

A Fill-Or-Kill order (FOK) is an order that must be filled immediately in its entirety. This means that there can be no partial execution of this order. This is beneficial when purchasing a large number of shares or purchasing a volatile stock. With partial execution with an order such as a market order, the investor can end up paying for more than the ask was originally priced at when they placed the position. If this order isn't filled within a few seconds, it is cancelled. Again, this gives an investor more control over price and execution than a normal market order.

Think of an immediate-or-cancel order as a FOK order except that it accepts partial execution of the position. Whereas in a FOK the entire order must be filled or cancelled, in an IOC order the position can be partially or completely filled with any remainder cancelled. This means that an investor has a greater chance of the order going through, though they may not get the full amount. IOC is another of the time in force order types along with GTC, FOK, and AON.

All-or-none orders are another of the time in force order types similar to FOK and IOC. With an AON order, the investor wants the entire position to be executed in its entirety, without partial execution. Unlike a FOK or IOC order, AON orders can stay open for a longer period of time. This is especially the case when large amounts of stock are being purchased. In the case of illiquid

58

positions, some AON orders may go unfilled. The FOK order is a combination of the IOC and the AON, as it is an all-or-none order that will cancel if not filled immediately.

When an investor is working with a registered representative, there will be times when the RR makes decisions for the client depending on their arrangements and suitability. In a discretionary order, the RR is making a decision about either the action to be taken, the asset to be bought or sold, or the amount. Anything that does not fall within these categories is prohibited. An RR who has discretionary capabilities can usually exercise some leeway in how positions are managed. For example, an RR may set a limit or stop price on an order to meet the needs of a clients, even without that client's express permission. This will depend on the relationship as well as any stipulations between the client and the firm.

A non-discretionary order would be the opposite of a discretionary order. It is where the client decides on the action to be taken, as well as the asset and amount, without giving the RR the ability to make changes to the order that are not expressly agreed upon. RRs will of course offer advice, as that is their role, but they would need permission from the client before taking action in their portfolio. Most orders would be non-discretionary.

A solicited order would be the broker's idea. For example, the broker may see that a client's position in XYZ stock is looking overweighted compared to the rest of the portfolio. The broker may call the client and encourage them to sell some of their position. This would be a solicited order as it was the broker's idea. Unless the broker is able to exercise discretion, then they cannot make the trade without the permission of the client.

An unsolicited order is the opposite of a solicited order. In this case, the order is the client's idea. If the client instructs the RR to sell 20 shares of ABC at $55 or better GTC, then that is an unsolicited and non-discretionary order. If the client told the RR to sell 20 shares of ABC at whatever price the RR thinks appropriate, then that would be an unsolicited but non-discretionary order, as the RR can determine a price for the order. These can be mixed and matched, as long as FINRA rules are being followed.

BUY AND SELL, BID-ASK

The bid and the ask prices of a security reflect the market for that asset. The bid is what buyers want to purchase at, and the ask is what sellers want to sell at. Remember that this is reflective of the secondary market, where things like liquidity and supply and demand can affect the bid and ask prices. When an investor goes into the market and purchases a stock, they will be purchasing at the ask, hopefully as low as possible. When a seller goes to sell a position, then they will be selling at the bid, hopefully as high as possible. The difference between the bid and ask prices is referred to as the **spread**. This spread is considered "tight" when the bid and ask are close together, or "wide" when they are far apart. Illiquid assets tend to have wider bid-ask spreads as they have less trading volume. Examples of illiquidity would be penny stocks, small cap stocks, trading after hours, etc.

A market maker is an institution at an exchange like the NYSE that serves to provide liquidity to the market. If no one else is buying, then the MM will, and the same goes for selling. MMs make their money off of the spread. Spreads are normally shown like this: 10.00 x 10.25, with the bid on the left and the ask on the right. The MM will sell at the ask and buy at the bid, thus making money off the spread, unlike investors. This may not seem like a lot, as it is usually just pennies, but when you are making hundreds of thousands of trades in volume, it adds up. Some MMs may pay brokers to route their customer's orders to them. This is called payment for order flow. It is allowable so long as the customer gets the best available price in the market.

TRADE CAPACITY

Firms can take on different roles in a trade depending on their size and the order. Not all BDs are big enough to have their own clearing firms or inventory for all trades. They may route customer's orders to clearing firms to be settled or buy shares out in the market. When a BD is acting in their principal capacity, then they are selling the shares out of their own inventory to the customer. This is the same function as a market maker. When a BD acts in this capacity they are going to charge a markup or a markdown on the order in lieu of a commission since they already own the stock. A firm cannot act as both agent and principal in the same trade.

When a broker does not have the inventory for a trade and must first purchase the shares before selling them to their customer, then they are acting in an agent capacity. In this instance, they would charge a commission to the customer instead of a markup or markdown. This can get rather complicated as the agent has to find someone willing to buy or sell at the counterparty's specifications. This could even be customers at other brokerage firms. This is one of the reasons orders may not be filled instantaneously. Remember that a BD cannot act as both agent and principal in one trade.

LONG AND SHORT POSITIONS

Long positions refers to purchasing an asset or security. When you buy stock in the market you are "long" on the stock. You want the price to appreciate so that you can make more money. There are many ways to be long on a stock other than simply purchasing shares; you can open options positions like long calls or use short puts to make extra income if the stock moves up. Long and short positions are related and are called opposite sides of the market. When a long position is increasing in value, the opposing short position is losing value. There are also long calls, which appreciate in value when the underlying decreases.

A short position is one in which the investor wishes for the underlying to depreciate in price, thus generating a return off the downside movement. Short positions are established by borrowing shares from a broker, selling them, and attempting to purchase them back at a lower price, thus pocketing the difference. It is important to remember that short positions are subject to unlimited loss. This is since a stock can theoretically go upwards to infinity and the short seller would be forced to buy back the shares at that price. This can be mitigated by purchasing a call option in order to cap the potential loss at the strike of the call.

NAKED AND COVERED POSITIONS

Naked or uncovered positions are established when the investor sells a call or put without the required stock or cash to cover the position. You are essentially agreeing to sell stock that you do not own. These are very risky as they subject the writer of the position to unlimited risk. Most accounts will not allow investors to place these trades. There are few instances where a naked call or put would make sense, if any.

Covered positions are when an investor sells a call or put and does own the required collateral, such as shares of the company or cash equivalents. This is much safer than an uncovered position. For a call to be covered, the writer of the option must hold 100 shares of the underlying in their account during the period that the option is in effect. For written puts, the investor will normally hold cash equivalent to purchasing 100 shares of the underlying at the strike of the contract. This way, if the writer is assigned, they have the necessary capital to cover the position, hence the name.

BEARISH AND BULLISH SENTIMENT

Bearish sentiment expects the market to depreciate. An investor with a bearish outlook on the market is planning and hoping that the market goes down over a certain period of time. Positions that tend to perform well in a bear market when prices are falling are long puts, short positions, covered calls, inverse ETFs, and a host of other positions and assets. A bear market is normally defined as when a broad market index such as the S&P 500 declines by 20% off its most recent high. Once that drop occurs, we are said to be in a "bear market."

Bullish sentiment is the opposite of bearish sentiment. Bulls expect the market to go up during a certain period of time. Bullish investors will likely hold long stock positions, long calls, short puts, and other asset classes that have a positive beta and tend to follow the overall trend of the market. Many times, roaring bull markets will follow a steep crash such as the "flash crash" during the beginning of the COVID-19 pandemic. However, past performance does not indicate future results. One can never guarantee the performance of an index, asset class, or anything else for that matter. Bullish sentiment bets that the market will go up, bearish sentiment bets it will go down.

INVESTMENT RETURNS

COMPONENTS OF RETURN

Interest income is a return paid to investors of income-based securities such as bonds. Bonds are the primary form of interest-bearing security, though there are many others such as a traditional CD one can get from their bank. Interest is normally paid out based on the coupon rate of a bond, which is a percentage of par value. Most bonds pay out in semi-annual installments. Other assets like CMOs and agency bonds may follow different schedules depending on the type. A bond bearing 8% will pay out $40 every six months. This interest income is normally taxed at an individual's ordinary income tax rate. Certain bonds carry preferential tax treatment, such as "munie" bonds which are normally tax-free at the federal level.

Dividends are paid out to certain common and preferred stockholders of corporations. Remember that stockholders do not have a right to a dividend; they only have a right to a dividend if declared by the board of directors. Dividends can be either cash or stock. Many stocks will pay a quarterly dividend, though this is not a rule. Some dividend investors will scale their investments such that they receive regular dividend payments every month. Dividends are more common in mature companies such as Coca-Cola or AT&T and less common with new and fast-moving growth companies. Investors tend to purchase blue-chip, mature equities for their dividends and relative safety, whereas they buy growth companies for the potential of capital appreciation and a surging stock price. Dividends vary from company to company, but tend to be a factor of a firm's EPS. Net income flows into the business and is then either reinvested into the business or paid out to shareholders in the form of a dividend.

Gains are realized when a position with an unrealized gain is sold and the gain is locked in. Realized gains are also referred to as capital gains as they are a return on an investor's capital separate from interest income. Short-term capital gains are when a position is sold for a gain after being held for a year or less. Long-term capital gains are where the position is sold after being held for over a year. Long-term capital gains are normally taxed at 15-20%, depending on the income of the individual or joint account. Short-term capital gains are taxed at an investor's ordinary income tax rate. There is clearly an incentive to hold positions for over a year in order to secure preferential tax treatment. Realized losses follow similar rules, and usually only $3,000 of capital losses can be deducted in a year, though rules will vary.

Unrealized gains are when a position has appreciated in value, but the position has not been closed. When a stock position appreciates by 10% but is not sold, that 10% is an unrealized gain on the position. Unrealized gains are not taxable, though there have been pushes to make them so, especially for billionaires. Once a position is sold and the gain locked it, it becomes a realized/capital gain and is taxable.

Return on capital/return on investment generally refers to the percentage return an investor makes on their capital or investment. If I invest $1,000 and I make $100, that is a 10% return or a 10% ROI. Total return is going to be the sum of any interest income or dividends received, as well as unrealized or realized gains. ROI is not the only way to measure an investment, as risk and exposure play a large role as well. Generally, investments with a higher average ROI will tend to carry greater risk.

Generally, the closer an individual is to retirement, the heavier weighted their portfolio will be towards income and interest-bearing securities. The younger an investor is, the more stock they will own and the more aggressive they will tend to be. The thought process behind this is that younger investors could sustain large losses, as they have many years ahead of them to earn more, whereas the closer you are to retirement, the less income-earning years you have ahead of you and the more important preservation of capital becomes. A portfolio geared towards income will be focused on bonds (government, municipal, corporate), and perhaps fixed-income or equity income mutual funds, high-yielding preferred stock, dividend paying companies as well as alterative assets such as CMOs. There are other ways to generate income, such as selling covered calls, though this may not always be suitable for investors. Growth portfolios will be focused on common stock such as emerging markets and growth companies.

TYPES OF DIVIDENDS

Cash dividends are the most common in the stock market. Usually, investors will receive a percentage of the market price of the stock or a percentage of the earnings per share. The dividend payout ratio is a function of the dividend divided by net income. It shows how much of a firm's net income is being paid out in the form of a dividend. You expect a higher dividend payout ratio from a mature, stable company than from a growth company. Most dividends are taxed as ordinary income, though some dividends qualify for special tax treatment (this is normally only available to institutional investors). For corporations, 50% of the cash dividend paid to the corporation from another corporation is 50% tax excludable.

Compared with a cash dividend, a stock dividend is where investors receive extra shares of the company in lieu of cash. This has the effect of increasing the number of common shares outstanding and usually diluting earnings per share. This means that a company's cash balance does not change, but share capital does. Stock dividends tend to be less common than cash dividends.

DIVIDEND PAYMENT DATES

When a corporation or fund's board of directors decides to pay a dividend to shareholders, the date they make the announcement is known as the declared date. This is the first important date in the cycle and begins the dividend payment cycle. Dividends will vary with whether the stock is preferred or common, as well as if it is cumulative or not. Remember that cumulative preferred stock has a special account associated with it known as "dividends in arrears" which is added too if a company misses a dividend. They must pay those preferred shareholders first before delivering a dividend to the common shareholders.

The ex-dividend date is the day the stock starts trading ex-dividend (Latin for "without"). On the ex-dividend date, the stock price will be adjusted downwards by the price of the dividend. For instance, if XYZ is trading at $25 prior to the ex-date and a $0.50 dividend is declared, then on the ex-date the stock will open at $24.50. The purpose for this is to keep investors from purchasing a security, receiving the dividend, and then selling it immediately after. Stocks trade regular way with a T+2. If an investor wants to receive the dividend, then they need to purchase the stock two days before the record date, which is one day before the ex-date. If the record date is on a Tuesday, the ex-date would be the preceding Monday, and the last day to buy the stock "cum-dividend" would be the Friday prior (since settlement only includes business days).

The record date is the date of record for stockholders who will receive the dividend. If an individual is not listed on the record date, then they will not receive the dividend. There is a prohibited practice known as "selling dividends" which occurs when an RR entices an investor to purchase a stock quickly in order to receive the dividend. This creates an artificial sense of urgency, sense the stock decreases by the dividend amount, and the investor would be taking on an unnecessary tax event in that situation.

The payable date is the last date in the dividend payment cycle and is set by the board of directors. It is the day that the taxable event occurs for an investor. If a dividend is declared in one tax year but payable in the next, then it would be taxed in the later tax year. The payable date is normally a few weeks after the date of record. As long as investors are on the books as of the record date, then they will receive the dividend on the payable date.

For a normal corporation, every date in the dividend cycle is set by the board of directors except for the ex-date, which is set by FINRA. This gives us the DERP mnemonic (Declared date, Ex-date, Record date, Payable date). This is not true however for a mutual fund. Mutual funds are able to set the ex-date for their shares since they do not trade on the secondary market. In the case of a mutual fund, the ex-date is set for one business day after the record date, which gives us the mnemonic DREP (Declared date, Record date, Ex-date, Payable date).

CONCEPTS OF MEASUREMENT

The yield on a bond usually refers to the stated coupon, which is what the bond pays in interest to the bearer, usually semi-annually. An 8% coupon on a par $1000 bond would give an investor $40 in interest every six months until maturity of the bond. However, this is not the only yield that a bond has; there are four main yields for most bonds, which are the current yield, the nominal yield, yield to call, and yield to maturity. These will change depending on the market and interest rates. A yield curve is a type of tool that graphs yields and maturities. A high-yield bond is usually referred to as a junk bond or speculative bond. These are normally not suitable for most investors.

Yield to maturity on a bond is essentially the percentage yield an investor would receive if they held the bond to maturity. Yield to maturity is affected by the market price of the bond as well as how many coupon payments are remaining until maturity. YTM is lower than the normal yield or current yield on a premium bond and higher than the YTC. The YTM is higher than the CY and NY on a discount bond and lower than the YTC.

A bond with a call provision can be called back by the issuer at a predetermined price and time. Bonds are likely to be called when interest rates are falling. When a bond is trading at a premium, then YTC should be what the RR quotes to the investor, as it is likely that it will be called. There is a concept known as yield to worst which means that the RR should quote the lower of either the YTM or YTC, thus being more realistic with what they present to the investor (as it is unlikely that you will be able to hold a steep premium bond to maturity).

Total return on a bond would be the sum of all coupons received as well as any capital gains on the bond if sold in the secondary market. Bonds issued at either a premium or discount trend towards par as they near maturity. Certain bonds must be accreted upwards when purchased at a discount or amortized downwards when purchased at a premium. This deals with potential capital gains and taxes if the bond is held to maturity. Certain bonds can also be converted into stock, which must also be factored into the potential return on the bond.

A basis point on a bond refers to 1/100ᵗʰ of a percentage point which is equivalent to 0.01% of par. The difference between 7.25% and 7.45% is 0.20% or 20 basis points or "bips." A basis point on a bond is equivalent to $10. Similar language is used for other fixed income securities as well as interest rates. Basis points are commonly used to refer to changes in the price of bonds.

The nominal yield on a bond is the stated rate of return per the coupon. Nominal yield is highest on a premium bond and lowest on a discount bond. If the coupon on a bond is 4% then that is also the nominal yield. The nominal yield does not change. Current yield on a bond is affected by the market price of the stock. Current yield can be thought of as a measure of what a bond pays you divided by what it costs you. A bond with a 4% coupon trading at par $1000 has a current yield of 4%, which is the same as the nominal yield. Where this will change is if the bond price shifts from par. Say the bond appreciates to $1100. Our new calculation is the 4% of $1000, which is our $40 annual interest income divided by the stepped-up market price of the bond at $1100. This gives us a new current yield of 3.63%, which is lower than the NY since this bond is trading at a premium. This helps to illustrate how the ROI on a bond will change as the price changes even though the interest payments do not.

COST BASIS REQUIREMENTS

Your cost basis on a position is what you originally bought it at. If someone dies and leaves stock to their children, then the children will inherit the stock at a stepped-up cost basis. Cost basis on stock will change if puts or calls are bought on the stock. A wash sale is when an investor sells a position at a loss for tax purposes and then purchases a like asset within 30 days. The IRS disallows the loss for that year. Appreciation in excess of cost basis becomes unrealized gains and price depression below cost basis becomes an unrealized loss.

BENCHMARKS AND INDICES

The S&P 500 is a standard benchmark in the securities industry. Most actively managed funds use it as a benchmark for their portfolios to beat. Other indices include the Dow, the NASDAQ, the Russel 2000, the Value Line Index, and the Wilshire 5000, among others. Managers attempt to generate an alpha return above a benchmark in order to justify their fees. For instance, if the S&P 500 return 8% on average, the fund might aim to return 10%, which would give them 2 percentage points of return in excess of a benchmark. At its most basic level, active portfolio management attempts to exceed a benchmark, whereas passive management seeks to merely match the performance of an underlying benchmark.

The DJIA is probably the most well-known index in the stock market. The index was created in 1896 and is comprised of 30 large-cap companies that trade on the NYSE and NASDAQ (this leads to the DJIA sometimes being referred to as the Dow 30). The Dow Jones Transportation Average is even older than the DJIA and is the original stock market index. The DJIA is price-weighted and contains companies in industrials, consumer goods, etc. The companies change over time as companies replace others in terms of market cap and growth. The DJIA should be used only as a proxy for the market and should be just one of many tools an investor has for analyzing the market. Since the DJIA contains such a small basket of stocks, many people prefer to look at the S&P 500 for a broader measure of the market.

The Standard and Poor's 500 index is possibly the most popular index for the U.S. stock market. It consists of 500 of the largest publicly traded companies in the country. It is market-cap weighted, meaning bigger companies like Apple will make up a bigger portion than smaller companies. There are many ETFs and mutual funds that track the S&P 500 or use it as a benchmark for performance. The S&P is heavily weighted in tech, as those companies tend to be some of the largest in the economy. The S&P 500, along with the Nasdaq and Dow, make up the most popular measures for the market.

The Nasdaq is both a trading system exchange and a series of indices. The Nasdaq Composite Index is the most popular of these and tracks smaller-cap companies that may not be listed on other indices, as well as large cap companies that are also on the S&P 500. There are over 3,700 stocks in the index, and it is market cap-weighted, similar to the S&P 500. Tech stocks account for roughly half of the Nasdaq which can cause greater volatility in the index since tech companies tend to be more volatile than other sectors and industries like industrials and consumer goods. In addition, about 40% of the total index is made up of just five mega-cap companies with Apple leading the way as of now. The Nasdaq serves as a good benchmark for tech and smaller cap companies since it is a broader measure than the S&P 500 or the DJIA.

The Russel 2000 tracks 2000 smaller companies that are also included in the Russel 3000. This index is considered a leading indicator for market performance as the smaller cap companies tracked by the index can be affected by changes sooner than large cap companies. Small cap mutual funds or ETFs tend to use the Russel 2000 as their benchmark as it more accurately reflects their intended performance.

The Wilshire 5000 index is one of the oldest broad-based measures of the U.S. investible market. Although it is called the Wilshire 5000, the number of companies can vary from 7,500 down to 3,500 as things ebb and flow. The index attempts to capture the entire investible market in the U.S. The companies included are every U.S. equity with readily available prices (bulletin-board issues not included). It is also market cap-weighted and is heavy in information technology, healthcare, and consumer discretionary. This index can serve as a good broad measure of the U.S. market.

The Value Line Index is interesting in that it covers North America equities, not just American. It is comprised of roughly 1,700 companies from the NYSE, Nasdaq, OTC markets, and Toronto exchanges. It has two separate components, the geometric composite index and arithmetic composite index. Value Line is a respected research firm and this index does a good job of reflecting the North American securities markets.

The CBOE Volatility Index (VIX) is a real time index that represents expectations for the strength of short-term price changes in the S&P 500. Prices are derived from S&P 500 index options and give us a picture of the volatility in the market. Generally, higher volatility is a bearish indicator and lower volatility is a bullish indicator. The VIX is also related to the price of options contracts as options are generally more expensive the more volatile they are. The VIX is a great tool for analyzing current investor sentiment and overall market volatility.

Treasury yields are a commonly used benchmark for the economy and representation of the bond market. Treasury yields refers to the yields on government bonds. Generally, the higher Treasury yields are, the less strong the equities market is. Also remember that bond prices and interest rates are inversely correlated. If the Fed raises rates, bond prices go down. The higher bond yields are, the more likely investors are to take money out of equities and park it in bonds. This gives us a roughly inverse relationship between Treasury yields and market performance.

TRADE SETTLEMENT

SETTLEMENT TIME FRAMES FOR VARIOUS PRODUCTS

Regular settlement for stocks as well as corporate and municipal bonds is T+2. If you execute an order on Monday, then it will settle on Wednesday (business days only). This is why dividends are only received by investors who purchase the stock regular way one day prior to ex. The same goes for corporate bonds and municipal bonds.

Regular way settlement for government securities is T+1. This means that a bond purchased on Monday will settle on Tuesday. These settle through the Federal Funds system. This is the same for Government Agency securities except for MBSs. This means your GNMAs, FHLMCs, and FNMAs all settle T+1 .

Similar to Government securities, options settle T+1. This means if you sell/buy an option on Wednesday, it will settle on Thursday. In certain cases, a customer can elect to use cash settlement for a position. Cash settles the same day as the trade, which can be advantageous for getting a stock before a dividend or similar instance. This gives us a framework of settlements: cash settles on T, options and govies settle T+1, equities, "Munies", and corporates settle T+2.

PHYSICAL VS. BOOK ENTRY

Physical delivery is exactly what it sounds like, the underlying asset is to be delivered to the purchaser on a specified delivery date. Before the internet, bonds and stocks would come in the form of physical certifications that the investor would keep or store in a bank. This is less secure generally than online means. Physical delivery now only relates to alternative investments like commodities. A related note is that some derivates can only settle for cash instead of the underlying asset. This is the case with ETFs, which will settle for cash instead of the underlying shares of the ETF.

Book-entry delivery and settlement is much more common, especially with online trading. Instead of issuing a physical certificate, the customer's name is merely added to the books for a company or removed, depending on if they are buying or selling. There are still some bonds, especially in Europe, where they are issued in bearer form to the buyer, but most securities in the U.S. will come fully registered and use book entry settlement and delivery.

CORPORATE ACTIONS
TYPES OF CORPORATE ACTIONS

A stock split, or forward stock split, occurs when an issuer splits shares into fractional shares. A common stock split might be a 2:1 stock split or a 3:2 stock split. This is merely an accounting measure and does not change the actual assets of the company nor affect the cost basis of the investor. What it does do is increase the amount of outstanding common shares, thus decreasing market price and earnings per share. It is important to be able to calculate the effects of a stock split. If an investor owns 100 shares of ABC at $50 and ABC does a 2:1 stock split, the investor will then have 200 shares at $25. Proportional ownership stays the same, market price goes down, and shares outstanding goes up. This is common for companies whose shares are very expensive.

A reverse stock split is essentially the opposite of a stock split. Instead of producing more shares at a lower price, a reverse stock split delivers less shares at a higher price. This is common for companies whose shares are very cheap, such as under $5, who may want to stay out of penny stock territory. A reverse stock split would be listed as a 1:2, 1:4, etc. If a customer has 100 shares of ABC at $50 and ABC does a 1:4 reverse stock split, the investor will be left with 25 shares of ABC at $200. This caused outstanding shares to decrease, market price to increase, and earnings per share to increase.

When a company executes a share buyback, they are purchasing shares from investors in the secondary market. These reacquired shares then become Treasury stock, which has no voting rights and pays no dividends. Companies may elect to do this because they have excess capital or because they believe their shares are undervalued. There are two ways a company can go about this; they can tender an offer directly to existing shareholders or purchase them from the open market.

A tender offer is an offer made to existing shareholders of a company's stock. Usually, tender offers are for share buybacks or when a company is issuing additional shares. If a company is issuing additional shares, they will normally offer rights to their existing shareholders, since common stockholders have the right to maintain proportional ownership. An investor can always take advantage of a tender offer or sell their shares in the open market to other buyers.

An exchange offer is when a firm offers to give one security for another security, hence the term exchange. This might occur when a firm offers another firm bonds for stock or vice versa. There are many different ways that this can be carried out. This can help avoid tax liability as it is essentially a trade of securities rather than purchasing and selling them on their own.

Rights are a form of equity security that have intrinsic value and are exercisable below the current market price of the stock. Rights will normally be issued when a company seeks to issue additional shares to the public and thus makes a rights offering to existing shareholders for them to maintain proportional ownership of the company. One right is issued for one share and several rights are needed to convert into a single share. It may be 5 rights for one share or 10 rights for one share or any number of options. The conversion price for the rights will be below the current market price of the stock, thus locking in a gain. Sometimes, fractional rights can be rounded up to purchase another share. An investor can exercise their rights or sell them in the secondary market. These are contrasted with warrants, which are long term and exercisable above the CMP. Rights are short term and typically expire within a few months.

A merger is when two or more companies merge together to form a new company whose leadership is made up of both companies. An acquisition is when one firm buys another. These are big deals and M&As are one of the main functions of bankers, as they can be worth millions upon millions. Anti-trust laws come into play here as a firm may gain an unfair advantage if they acquire all their competitors or if two competitors merge together (imagine if Apple merged with Microsoft or Tesla with Ford). These deals will usually be financed with a combination of cash, debt, and equity. If company A is buying company B, they may give company B cash from debt financing as well as shares in company A. This is a large and complex field that has a large impact on the market, as news of M&As can send a stock into a more volatile range.

A spinoff occurs when a company decides to take one element or division of their business and spin it off to be its own distinct entity. This happens often with large corporations or conglomerates. Sometimes these segments are sold to other businesses and sometimes they become publicly traded stocks themselves. When a company spins off a subsidiary, the investor will normally receive a percentage ownership in the new company. For example, if you hold 100 shares of ABC and they spin off a subsidiary worth 10% of the company, then you will be left with 90% ABC and 10% of the new subsidiary.

IMPACT OF STOCK SPLITS AND REVERSE STOCK SPLITS ON MARKET PRICE AND COST BASIS

A forward stock split gives us more shares at a lower market price, whereas the reverse stock split gives us fewer shares at a higher market price. CMP goes down in a forward stock split and goes up in a reverse stock split. Cost basis is a little more complicated. The IRS does not consider a stock split to be a taxable event as you have the exact same ownership percentage as you did before the split, just with a different quantity and price. In a stock split, your total cost basis does not change, but your per share cost basis does change. In a forward stock split, your per share cost basis will decrease, and in a reverse stock split it will increase. Stock splits and stock dividends can also affect orders like stop orders.

ADJUSTMENTS TO SECURITIES SUBJECT TO CORPORATE ACTIONS

To quickly recap how securities are affected by corporate actions: in a forward stock split you receive more stock at a lower cost basis; in a reverse stock split you receive fewer shares at a higher cost basis; in a cash dividend you receive cash in the form of a taxable event; in a stock dividend you receive more shares, which increases your ownership and may be taxed at capital gains levels (if qualified);a spinoff gives the investor shares in the spinoff in proportion to its allocation of the total company (e.g. a company spins off a subsidiary which is worth 5% of the company. If the investor had 100 shares originally, they will now have 95 in the parent and 5 in the spinoff.); mergers and acquisitions usually lead to an increase in the price of the stock (some companies are delisted when fully acquired and the investors may receive shares in the takeover company); buybacks decrease outstanding shares and increase treasury stock; rights offerings give existing owners the ability to subscribe to new shares at a discounted price; and warrants are added onto other deals that are exercisable over the CMP and are longer-term compared to rights.

DELIVERY OF NOTICES AND CORPORATE ACTION DEADLINES

There are a plethora of statements and notices that publicly-traded firms file with the SEC and make available to the public. The most important are the 10, 10Q, 8K, and proxies. The 10K is the annual statement and includes the all-important financials, including the income statement, balance sheet, and statement of cash flows. The 10Q is the quarterly version of the 10K and includes quarterly earnings. 8Ks are a type of current report and are only filed when there is a major event that stockholders should know about. Firms traditionally have 4 days to file a form 8K. Proxy statements are sent usually before board meetings and can serve as a good source of information about the company's current business.

PROXIES AND PROXY VOTING

Shareholders do not have to be present at a board meeting in order to vote. Most shareholders will vote by proxy, which means they will send in their votes ahead of time rather than going to the meeting in-person. A proxy statement is a document sent to shareholders, normally before an annual board meeting. It serves as an overview of important news and what may be discussed. This will provide investors with the information needed to make informed voting decisions.

Customer Accounts and Compliance Considerations

ACCOUNT TYPES AND CHARACTERISTICS

CASH

The most basic brokerage account would be an individual cash account. In a cash account, an investor must have 100% of the price of a transaction ready in the form of cash in their account in order to affect a trade. Margin is not allowed in a cash account. The most basic level of cash account only allows investors to purchase long positions. Accounts can be approved to trade options as long as they are covered rather than naked. Cash accounts cannot borrow, so they cannot sell short.

MARGIN

A margin account is like a cash account except there is borrowing allowed. This opens up many doors for the investor. It allows them to sell stock short, purchase leveraged products, open uncovered positions, and purchase shares on margin. Margin rules are subject to Reg T and minimum maintenance requirements. Margin is essentially credit borrowed from the brokerage like a loan. It carries an interest rate and subjects the investor to much greater risk than a traditional cash account.

Initial margin requirements are set by the FRB in Reg T. Initial margin is 50% of the value for short or long positions. Maintenance margin requirements differ depending on the firm or the security and FINRA. Traditionally, maintenance margin is 25% of long market value (LMV) or 30% of short market value (SMV). These can change and investors must constantly be aware of their debit or credit balances to make sure that they do not fall below maintenance margin and experience a margin call or maintenance call.

OPTIONS

Accounts that can trade options come in a few levels. First, investors must be found suitable for options trading and must receive the options agreement and the options disclosure document detailing the risks involved. Level one options trading involves selling covered calls and cash-secured or covered puts. There is minimal risk involved with these strategies as they are not subject to unlimited risk. Level two options trading opens the door to long calls, long puts, and strategies made up of those trades including strangles and straddles. At this level, the most an investor can lose is the premium paid for a position. Level three options trading includes spreads, which is buying and selling options at different prices and expirations. Finally, level four trading allows investors to write naked options, which subjects the investor to potential unlimited risk if uncovered by another option contract. This is normally only suitable for sophisticated investors.

DISCRETIONARY VS. NON-DISCRETIONARY

A non-discretionary account is the standard for most new accounts. This means that only the investor who owns the account has the right and ability to buy and sell securities as well as add and withdraw funds. Some investors will have power of attorney given to a relative, like a child, in which case they could also have that authority inherent in the account. A discretionary account is where the RR can control asset, action, and price with the goodwill of the investor. This means the RR can not only recommend trades but also affect trades in the account. There are rules that regulate what the RR can and cannot do, and they must act in the best interests of their client.

FEE-BASED VS. COMMISSION

Prior to the advent of commission-free trading through brokerages such as Robinhood, most brokerages charged commission on trades both opening and closing. This means an investor that made frequent trades could find themselves spending large sums of money just on commission. Many accounts still have commission trading in place, depending on the brokerage and products advisor. A fee-based account is usually associated with an investment advisor who charges a flat fee, usually based off the assets in the account. Brokerages should aim to put customers in accounts that are most suitable for their needs without attempting to maximize fees.

A wrap account is a special type of account where defined fees cover all of the brokerage and administrative expenses associated with the account. This type of account is professionally managed and the benefit comes when the flat fee ends up being less than the expenses associated with a regular account. If the investor is not fully using the wrap account and could save money using a different account, it is the responsibly of the RR to make them aware. The fees are usually a percentage of assets under management for the account. Wrap accounts are typically best suited for investors with high trading activity.

EDUCATIONAL ACCOUNTS

A few states have Education Savings Accounts that serve as a sort of supplement to a 529 plan and allow for savings to be accumulated for education-related expenses. ESAs can also be opened through brokers. A custodial brokerage account is an account set up for a minor, usually by the parent. Distributions are tax-free when used for eligible expenses. The Coverdell ESA is an example of one of these accounts at the federal level.

CUSTOMER ACCOUNT REGISTRATIONS

INDIVIDUAL

An individual brokerage account is one where there is a single owner of the account. There are both individual margin accounts and individual cash accounts. Individuals that are married and filing jointly can still open an individual account, but they can also open a joint account. The individual account is the most basic level of account.

JOINT

A joint account is usually opened by married couples. There are joint brokerage accounts just like there are joint bank accounts. For SIPC insurance purposes, joint accounts are considered separate from individual accounts (but individual cash and margin accounts are considered the same and are lumped together). Openers of a joint account do not have to be married; they could be relatives, friends, or business partners, though if there is a falling out it can lead to trouble with the account. If there is a divorce or similar separation, then the RR should wait before taking any action in the account such as liquidating and allowing one individual to cash out.

CORPORATE/INSTITUTIONAL

Many corporations open accounts to hold securities with broker-dealers. Since these are non-natural entities, specific procedures are required when opening the account. Specifically, the RR typically needs to receive a copy of the corporate charter and resolution. These documents will specify who is given trading authorization over the account. There are also more nuanced tax implications in an entity account, so financial advisors or tax professionals are especially beneficiary for corporations that want to open a brokerage account.

TRUST

In its simplest form, a trust is a type of legal entity that allows someone to manage someone else's money as a third party. The trust is set up independent of the brokerage account and requires its own slew of legal paperwork and documentation. In brokerage accounts, the first party is always the broker-dealer themselves. The second party is the person who owns the account and whose name is under it. The second party can give third party trading authorization to a third party in the case of a trust account (in a way similar to custodial accounts). A trust can be either revocable or irrevocable, which is rather self-explanatory. Revocable trusts can have the authorization amended or removed at the behest of the second party. On death, the beneficiary's assets go to their estate. An irrevocable trust cannot be amended. To open a trust agreement, BD's will require a copy of the trust agreement and supporting documentation.

CUSTODIAL

In the United States, anyone under the age of 18 cannot technically legally own assets or securities. If a parent or guardian wishes to setup an account for their child, they must setup a custodial account. There are two main types of custodial accounts: UTMAs (Uniform Transfer to Minors Act) and UGMAs (Uniform Gift to Minors Act). These accounts are setup under the SSN of the minor with the custodian acting as the manager of the account. UTMA accounts can hold a wider variety of assets than UGMAs. Custodial accounts can be created at brokerages, banks, and other finance companies. Transfers or contributions are not taxable (any contributions over 16k are taxable as gifts) or revocable. Depending on state laws, the custodian will take over the account when they come of age (18-25).

PARTNERSHIPS

Partnerships are a type of legal entity similar to an LLC or corporation. There are many types of partnerships, such as limited and limited liability partnerships. Partnerships may wish to setup an account with a broker. To do this, the broker will require a copy of the partnership resolution. In either a normal partnership or limited partnership, gains and losses will flow through to the partners, similar to DPPs. In a normal partnership, the partners are jointly and severally liable for any and all debts of the partnership; in a limited partnership, there is the GP who manages and who bears unlimited liability and the LPs who provide capital and are only liable up to their original investment. For partnerships, most brokerages offer both cash and margin accounts.

RETIREMENT

The traditional IRA is a popular investment vehicle that allows the owner to save for retirement independent of their employer. IRAs have a max contribution of $6,500 a year as of the 2023 tax year. This increases to $7,500 if the owner is 50 or older. IRA contributions grow tax-deferred, meaning the owner will owe ordinary income tax on any distributions once they hit retirement age at 59 ½. The thought process is that the investor's tax bracket will be lower in retirement than in their working years, allowing them to save money on taxes as well as save for retirement. If the investor is not already covered under an employer tax-qualified plan like a 401k or 403b, then the investor's personal contribution to the IRA is tax deductible, thus lowering their taxable income. You can still make a contribution if covered under an employer plan, it just won't be tax deductible. The investor can contribute to both a Roth IRA and traditional IRA as long as they do not exceed the $6,500/$7,500 combined annual contribution limit. Required minimum distributions (RMDs) are required once the investor reaches 72.

The main difference between a Roth IRA and traditional IRA is their tax treatment. In a Roth IRA, contributions are not tax-deductible but they grow tax-free. Contributions are made with after-tax dollars, and any gains made in the account held until retirement age are exempt from tax. This is a very significant advantage and partly due to the fact that Roth IRAs are not open to high-income earners (as of the 2023 tax year, that is $153,000 for individuals and $228,000 for joint filers). Similar rules around contributions relate to Roth IRAs as to traditional IRAs. You can contribute to a Roth IRA even if covered by a 401k.

A company defined benefit plan is rare in today's economy. These are more commonly known as pension plans. They pay out to an employee a set amount, usually based on how much they earned at the company. The longer you work for the company and the more you earn, the greater your pension. These still exist in many government jobs and the military but are virtually non-existent in America's private market. The employers contribute to this plan, and the employee will receive a fixed amount at retirement. These are now largely replaced by the 401k.

The 401k is now the most common employer-sponsored retirement plan. They are also known as defined contribution plans since contributions are made by the employee instead of the employer as in a defined contribution plan. Some employers will match a certain percentage of their employee's contributions, but not always. 401ks are covered by ERISA laws similar to 403bs and pension plans. 401k contributions are made with pre-tax dollars and thus grow tax deferred. The investor will pay ordinary income tax rates on qualified distributions made from the 401k in retirement. There is also a 10% early withdrawal penalty for distributions made before 59 ½ unless used for certain qualifying events.

SEP (Simplified Employee Pension) IRAs are available to any sized business, even self-employed owners. These are cheaper to start and operate and allow for a contribution of up to 25% of total pay for individuals. The contributions are flexible, which is beneficial for businesses that may struggle with cash flow issues. Contributions must also be equal for all employees (based off percentages of total compensation). There are also zero filing requirements for businesses who elect the SEP IRA, making it that much more attractive.

The SIMPLE (Savings Incentive Match PLan for Employees) IRAs is ideal for small businesses that do not currently offer a retirement plan. These are generally only available to businesses with 100 or fewer employees. This is more closely related to a 401k, whereas the SEP IRA is more like a pension plan. Employers must make either a matching contribution or minimum contribution to an employee's plan annually. Due to their "simple" nature, SIMPLE IRAs are a popular alternative to the 401k for small businesses.

Think of a 403b as a 401k for non-profits, as that is the main difference. 403b accounts are only available to non-profits and are commonly offered by public schools as well as 501(c)(3) nonprofit organizations. The function like a 401k, since employees make contributions to the account with employers able to contribute as well. These accounts are sometimes stricter in their investment options when compared to normal 401ks. The employer will have to select appropriate investment options that will be made available to employees.

Keogh plans, also known as HR-10 plans, are a relatively obsolete type of retirement account for self-employed individuals. They function like a tax-deferred pension plan. They can be a defined contribution plan like a 401k or a defined benefit plan like a SEP IRA. They are also used by unincorporated businesses. It is unlikely that you will run into this term much in the current market since they have largely been replaced by 401ks, SEP IRAs, and SIMPLE IRAs.

REQUIRED MINIMUM DISTRIBUTIONS

A required minimum distribution (RMD) is a rule placed on certain retirement accounts that stipulate how much money must be taken out of the accounts at certain times. RMDs are normally in effect for tax-qualified plans whose investments grow tax-deferred. This means when the investor decides to withdraw money, they will owe ordinary income tax on the distributions. RMDs are in place for tradition IRAs but not Roth IRAs. This is because Roth IRA distributions are not taxable. The IRS does not care when you take money out of a Roth IRA since they won't see any of it, whereas they want to be able to tax your traditional IRA. For the traditional IRA, RMDs must take place once the holder reaches the age of 72 (adjusted upwards from 70 ½ as of 2019/2020). The exact RMD will vary as it is dependent upon both life expectancy and the age of the investor. RMDs are generally associated with defined contribution plans, as well as SEP IRAs and SIMPLE IRAs.

CONTRIBUTIONS

Usually, when an account has some sort of tax advantage to it, then there will be a limit on annual contributions. As of 2023, the max annual contribution to an IRA or Roth IRA combined is $6,500, or $13,000 if married and filing jointly. For the 401k, 403b, SEP IRA, and SIMPLE IRA, the max contributions depend on the employee's income, the tax year, the employee's age, and can also be subject to cost of living adjustments. The most testable thing to remember is the current $6,500/$13,000 max annual contribution on IRAs and Roth IRAs. Remember you can contribute to both a traditional and Roth IRA; it just cannot exceed the annual limit when combined.

ANTI-MONEY LAUNDERING (AML)

DEFINITION OF MONEY LAUNDERING

Money laundering is the illegal practice of mixing cash made through illegal activities (e.g., narcotics, trafficking, etc.) into legitimate businesses in order to make the "dirty" money look like "clean" money that can be taxed and withdrawn from the business. Money laundering is an essential part of most criminal enterprises, most commonly in the sale of illegal drugs. When you have cash from an illegal activity, you cannot simply go down and deposit it in the bank without raising questions from the IRS and risking an audit. So, what criminals do is buy businesses (generally cash businesses like laundromats, car washes, etc.) and inject their dirty money into the business. They will then take various actions to overstate expenses or other activities of the business, possibly by creating fake invoices for purchases that never happened or overstating the cost of improvements or equipment. This gives accounting room for the dirty money to fill the gap between the clean money made by the business legally and the overstated expenses/profits. The dirty money can then be withdrawn from the business.

STAGES OF MONEY LAUNDERING

The three stages of money laundering are placement, layering, and integration. The first step, placement, is where the dirty money generated through illegal means is injected into the legitimate business or accounts. The money might be shuffled through different accounts and even exchanged through different currencies in an attempt to make it virtually untraceable. The next stage of layering is when this dirty money is mixed with the clean money to the point where no one can tell what is dirty and what is clean. This is where purchasing and invoicing might come into play, as well as wire transfers and purchasing of assets and taking out loans. After placement and layering have been completed successfully, integration takes place. This is where the money laundering is complete. The dirty money is now completely mixed with the clean money and can be withdrawn from the business through various means such as wages, salaries, or other investments.

AML COMPLIANCE PROGRAM

Anti-Money Laundering (AML) rules are in place to catch would-be money launderers and to protect financial institutions from becoming complicit in the illegal activity. Many money launderers use brokerage accounts to buy assets or transfer money, which makes AML compliance all the more important. Basic AML requirements are the creation of written procedures and policies that must be followed, as well as the designation of an AML compliance officer for the firm. It can also include risk assessment, training programs, and auditing. Ultimately, the goal is to catch any potential illegal activities as soon as possible. The SAR and CTR are tools that are used to alert FinCEN of any potential illegal activities.

SUSPICIOUS ACTIVITY REPORT (SAR)

A Suspicious Activity Report (SAR) is a type of report that is filed with FinCEN by financial institutions. It is used when the company suspects that actions taken by clients may be indicative of illegal activities. The rules regulating the use of the SAR are related to the Bank Secrecy Act (BSA). A SAR must be filed if cash transactions exceed $10,000 in a day for an account/customer in the aggregate. They may also be filed for suspicious activity that the company suspects is related to illegal activities.

CURRENCY TRANSACTION REPORT (CTR)

A Currency Transaction Report (CTR) is similar to a SAR in that it is filed with FinCEN and is used by financial institutions to report suspicious activity. CTRs must also be filed when daily currency transactions exceed $10,000. They are considered less far-reaching, as SARs can be filed based off

suspicion even if the $10,000 limit is not breached. Criminals know that $10,000 will trigger a CTR, so they will structure their withdrawals or transfers to come in under the limit. If a financial institution notices this, they can still file a SAR. Combined, these reports allow companies to help catch and stop illegal activities.

FinCEN

The Financial Crimes Enforcement Network (FinCEN) serves as a bureau underneath the U.S. Department of the Treasury and exists to monitor and stop financial crimes. The SAR and CTR are both filed with FinCEN. FinCEN operates under various laws and regulations including the legislative framework of the Bank Secrecy Act and PATRIOT Act. FinCEN supports law enforcement and serves as a way to manage and synthesize information while monitoring potential threats.

OFFICE OF FOREIGN ASSET CONTROL (OFAC) AND THE SPECIALLY DESIGNATED NATIONALS AND BLOCKED PERSONS (SDNS)

The Office of Foreign Asset Control (OFAC) is another section underneath the U.S. Department of the Treasury. The mission of OFAC is to enforce trade and economic sanctions against foreign countries, as dictated by the government. As part of this mission, OFAC publishes lists of individuals and companies that are either working for or owned by foreign target governments or connected to terrorist organization. One of these lists is the Specially Designated Nationals (SDN) list, as well as the Consolidated Sanctions list.

BOOKS AND RECORDS AND PRIVACY REQUIREMENTS

BOOKS AND RECORDS RETENTION REQUIREMENTS

Since the financial industry is heavily regulated, there are specific requirements for how long different documents such as trade statements, account statements, etc. must be retained. An applicable rule is SEA Rule 17a-4(b)(4), which states the BDs must retain all related business communication, either received or sent, for three years, the first two of which must be kept in what is considered an easily accessible place. The retention period for most statements relating to the customer is six or three years, though it may vary.

CONFIRMATIONS AND ACCOUNT STATEMENTS

Under FINRA rule 4511 any records that do not have a defined retention period must be held for a minimum of six years. Customer confirmations and account statements are partly regulated under SEA Rule 17a, which states that the retention period for customer accounts statements as well as trade confirmations must also be held for a minimum of six years (the first two of which must be in an easily accessible place. When in doubt, go for six years.).

HOLDING OF CUSTOMER MAIL

Traditionally, BDs will send customers statements monthly in physical format. Customers can elect to have their statements delivered electronically if they wish. FINRA states that customer mail can be held for up to three months for any reason. It may be because the customer is moving, out of the country, etc. This is covered under Rule 3150. BDs are allowed to hold the mail as long as they received written instructions from the customer, have informed them of other delivery options, and are still able to communicate with the customer.

BUSINESS CONTINUITY PLANS (BCP)

FINRA Rule 4370 lays out the framework for business continuity plans in use by BDs. Essentially, FINRA requires BDs to write BCPs that establish how they will meet their obligations to their customers and other firms. These are usually updated regularly. These BCPs need to be rather detailed as they will examine different market conditions and situations and how the company will respond to it. BCPs can serve as a form of risk management and mitigation.

CUSTOMER PROTECTION AND CUSTODY OF ASSETS

As part of their normal course of business, BDs normally hold customers' assets for them. FINRA clearly stipulates that the firm must safeguard these securities and keep them easily accessible. This means that the firm must keep those customer assets separate from their proprietary operations and must deliver them upon request of the customer. When it comes to margin, customer's fully paid securities must be held separate from marginable securities. To do otherwise would jeopardize the customer's assets.

PRIVACY REQUIREMENTS

Given the nature of BDs operations with customers and the sensitive data they have on file, FINRA sets clear rules on privacy and safeguarding requirements for customer's data. Regulation S-P gives guidance on this subject. The regulation states that BDs must have written procedures in place for how to maintain the integrity of customer data and how it will be protected from potential hazards. BDs are also required to deliver initial as well as annual privacy disclosures to customer's detailing these protections as well as data use. On top of this, Regulation S-ID requires that BDs who govern covered accounts create and maintain an identity theft protection program.

COMMUNICATIONS WITH THE PUBLIC AND GENERAL BEST INTEREST OBLIGATIONS AND SUITABILITY REQUIREMENTS

COMMUNICATIONS WITH THE PUBLIC AND TELEMARKETING

Telemarketing and cold calling have long been a part of prospecting for broker-dealers. In the advent of legislation like the Telemarketing Sales Rule and the 1994 Telemarketing and Consumer Fraud and Abuse Prevention Act define rules that BDs and other sales companies must abide by when engaging in telemarketing. Generally, telemarketing is only allowed between the hours of 8 a.m. and 9 p.m. in the time zone of the person being called. FINRA Rule 3230 establishes these rules for BDs. The main rules are that the 8-9 rule can be broken if the firm has a preexisting relationship with the prospect/customer and that the firm must maintain a Do-Not-Call list in addition to the National DNC list.

BEST INTEREST OBLIGATIONS AND SUITABILITY REQUIREMENTS

In the context of advising and related services, BDs have a fiduciary responsibility to keep their customer's best interests first and foremost. These are codified as Know-Your-Customer (KYC) rules, which lay out some rules for customer recommendations and suitability. Rule 2090 establishes these provisions. Essentially, KYC boils down to doing due diligence on customer recommendations and accounts. For instance, BDs should not "churn" a customer's account to generate excessive fees, engage in the trading of mutual fund shares, make blanket recommendations for speculative investments such as penny stocks, or only perform suitability analyses for one or two customers. Remember the difference between a solicited (BD recommendation) and unsolicited (customer's idea) order. Know your customer and avoid a lawsuit.

Prohibited Activities

MARKET MANIPULATION

DEFINITION OF MARKET MANIPULATION

Broadly speaking, market manipulation is when one or more parties engage in activities with the goal of affecting the price of a security. Common forms of market manipulation would be illegal activities like spoofing or front-running positions. Another activity that could be construed as market manipulation is when an institution seeks to purchase a large block of shares shortly before close. Advisors have a responsibility to inform customers of any activities that could be seen as market manipulation. Other forms of market manipulation could be spreading rumors to affect stock prices.

TYPES OF MARKET MANIPULATION

Market rumors are exactly what they sound like: spreading rumors in order to change the price of the stock. If someone has a sizable short position on a company, they might spread negative information about the firm in order to cause other investors to sell, thereby driving the price down. Market rumors are common with celebrities or firms that have large audiences and could drastically affect a stock with a mere mention or tweet. A pump and dump is one of the oldest forms of market manipulation in the book. Investors will get into an investment (normally a very speculative one) and load up on their positions. As the next stage of the scheme, they will spread hype for the company or security thereby causing other investors to pile onto the investment "pumping" the price up. This normally takes place on investments with low outstanding shares or limited supply, thus making them more vulnerable to sudden increases in price. Finally, the original investors will sell all at the same time at the new high price causing the asset to plummet thus the "dump". The other investors are left with a worthless position. The pump and dump has been happening frequently in the crypto space.

Front running is a form of insider trading. Say that you're an advisor at a broker-dealer. You are at your desk and overhear a conversation from your coworker's cubicle. You hear that your coworker's large institutional client is preparing to purchase a very large position in a company (large enough to affect the stock price). You then take this information, and either purchase shares in the company yourself or call your customers and tell them to buy the company immediately. Thus, you are front running the institutional order and will experience a gain when their order goes through. This is considered market manipulation and is prohibited.

In fee or commission-based accounts where the customer is charged for each trade, there can exist a misalignment of incentives where the RR may execute excessive trades in order to generate more commissions from them. This is prohibited since it is not in the best interest of the customer. RR must abide by KYC rules and act in their best interest. RRs also have a responsibility to ensure the customer has the account that best meets their needs. For instance, if a customer has an account that generates higher fees due to certain privileges but is not using them, it may be beneficial for them to be moved to a lower fee account. It goes back to doing what is best for the customer.

Marking the open or close is a prohibited practice where an investor (either institutional or individual) seeks to purchase a security prior to close or open with the purpose of influencing the stock price upwards in order to turn a quick profit. Stocks are volatile towards open and close, and if a large order comes through during these times it can have an outsized affect as other investors follow. RRs have a responsibility to inform their clients if any of their trades could be construed as market manipulation in the form of marking the open or close (i.e., an institutional client should not place a very large buy order five minutes before close).

Backing away is a prohibited practice where a market maker fails to honor a previously made quote. MMs provide liquidity in capital markets by buying at the bid and selling at the ask. If a market maker gives a firm quote for a stock at $10.25 and refuses to honor it, this is called backing away as they are backing away from their quote. This can happen in other security transactions as well between broker-dealers. Firm quotes must be honored, otherwise the firm is engaged in backing away and could be subject to disciplinary action.

In an individual cash account an investor must pay for a security before selling it (for obvious reasons). Free riding occurs when an investor purchases a security and then turns around and sells it before payment clears. This violates the Fed's Reg T and can cause that account to be frozen for 90 days (this is different than the wash sale rule). When an account is frozen, securities can still be purchased but they must be paid in full before being sold.

INSIDER TRADING

DEFINITION OF INSIDER TRADING

Insider trading is an illegal activity where investors utilize what is called "material non-public information" in order to make money on the trading of securities. An example of this would be the CEO shorting his company's stock before they announce poor quarterly earnings. Insiders are considered anyone who is an executive/officer of the business (CEO, CFO, Chief Counsel, Accounting Firm, etc.), a principal stockholder, or a nuclear relative of those individuals. Material non-public information is any information that is not available to the public and has the capacity to affect stock prices. Someone who gives out insider information is considered a tipper, and the receiver is considered a tippee. Violators of insider trading are subject to treble damages (3x). If an individual makes $1 million from insider trading, they are subject to paying $3 million in damages.

DEFINITION OF MATERIAL NONPUBLIC INFORMATION

Material non-public information is information that is not publicly available ("insider information") and has the ability to affect stock prices (e.g., earnings reports could affect the stock price, but news that the CEO just bought a jet probably wouldn't). There are many safeguards kept in place to keep insider information from being leaked and used for illegal gains. Insiders are normally barred from certain trading activities. There are also information walls setup within firms that have consumer investment departments, investment banking departments, and any groups that could have access to material non-public information.

IDENTIFYING INVOLVED PARTIES

Involved parties are individuals or institutions who would be considered insiders. According to the SEC, involved parties are "officer, director, 10% stockholder and anyone who possesses inside information because of his or her relationship with the Company or with an officer, director or principal stockholder of the Company." An individual who owns 10% of the company's outstanding shares would still be considered an insider even if they are not employed by the firm (since they are considered an owner). SEC Rule 10b-5 is the rule that prohibits insider trading with respect to involved parties. Insiders normally have to go through special avenues in order to trade the company's stock.

PENALTIES

Insider trading is a very damaging business as it can cause losses for those that are not involved in the insider trading. Insider trading is subject to treble damages, which means that triple the gains will be assessed in fines. Insider trading and other securities related fraud can result in not only expulsion from the firm (if an employee) but even incarceration in federal prison. Anytime material non-public information is leaked, the company must file with the SEC as soon as possible to limit liability. Most insider trading is caught sooner rather than later. If someone becomes aware of MNPI they should alert the authorities immediately.

OTHER PROHIBITED ACTIVITIES

RESTRICTIONS PREVENTING ASSOCIATED PERSONS FROM PURCHASING INITIAL PUBLIC OFFERINGS (IPOS)

Under FINRA Rule 5130 associated persons are prohibited from engaging in the purchase of Initial Public Offerings in any account that they have a beneficial interest in. This includes direct relatives of the associated person (e.g., dependent children, spouse, etc.). They are also prohibited from purchasing IPOs. This is due to insider trading laws.

USE OF MANIPULATIVE, DECEPTIVE OR OTHER FRAUDULENT DEVICES

FINRA rule 2020 prohibits RRs from engaging in the sale of securities or any business through the use of manipulative, deceptive, or fraudulent devices. This is pretty straightforward. It goes in line with the KYC rules as well as RRs responsibilities to keep their customer's interests first and foremost. These "devices" could be aggressive sales tactics or illegal practices like backing away, front running, etc. RRs should always act in the best interests of their customers, and things will normally go well for them.

IMPROPER USE OF CUSTOMERS' SECURITIES OR FUNDS

FINRA rule 2150 overviews the improper use of customers' securities and funds. First, RRs are prohibited from improperly using customer funds. RRs are also prohibited from guaranteeing a customer account against loss (they can recommend the use of certain strategies to reduce risk, like hedging, but cannot guarantee against loss). In the area of sharing in customer gains and losses, RRs are allowed to share in a customer account as long as written permission is received from both customer and member firm, and the gains are shared in direct proportion to the capital invested by both RR and customer (i.e., if the RR's money makes up 50% of the account, then they can share in 50% of the gains).

FINANCIAL EXPLOITATION OF SENIORS

Member firms have a responsibility not only to not exploit seniors but also to prevent them from being exploited by others using their account. Member firms should take actions to obtain a trusted contact person's information and have the ability to freeze a customer's account if they believe that they are being exploited. FINRA rule 2165 establishes these allowances. There are ongoing analyses of what actions a BD should be allowed to take in the interest of seniors. Regulatory Notice 19-36 is once such request.

ACTIVITIES OF UNREGISTERED PERSONS

Unregistered persons are normally clerical employees of a member firm (as opposed to sales staff or other registered representatives). Clerical employees are unregistered and are only permitted to engage in administrative tasks. They can help customers with items such as delivering forms but cannot solid orders nor make recommendations, as they are not qualified to do so. This protects both firm, employee, and customer. Unregistered persons are also unable to receive commissions.

FALSIFYING OR WITHHOLDING DOCUMENTS

Falsifying or withholding documents is criminal and illegal. They are violations of FINRA rule 2010, which lays out many rules for commercial honor and principles of trade. Given the important nature of the financial industry, it is essential that documents are kept safe and are not tampered with. Member firms must ensure the safety and security of these documents.

PROHIBITED ACTIVITIES RELATED TO MAINTENANCE OF BOOKS AND RECORDS

As with other restrictions on books and records, member firms are prohibited from either falsifying documents or improperly maintaining them. There will be different rules for record keeping depending on the firm and the type of communication (electronic mail, paper mail, fax, etc.). Failure to properly maintain documents can result in disciplinary action, including the possibility of fines.

Overview of the Regulatory Framework

SRO Regulatory Requirements for Associated Persons

REGISTRATION AND CONTINUING EDUCATION

SRO QUALIFICATION AND REGISTRATION REQUIREMENTS

Broker-dealers are required to register with an SRO (usually FINRA) in order to do business. BDs are also required to register in any state which they do business (either having an office in state or clients who reside in state). Essentially, any firm or person who is involved in the marketing and selling of securities in either a broker or dealer capacity is required to register with an SRO. Brokers are those firms which effect transactions in the securities market. Dealers are those who buy and sell securities for their own account. It is testable to remember that a firm is operating in a broker basis when acting as an agent, whereas they operate as a dealer when acting in a principal capacity.

DEFINITION OF REGISTERED VS. NON-REGISTERED PERSON

A registered person is an individual who is registered with the SRO responsible for their field of work. This includes officers, principals, associates, managers, etc. Registered persons (which includes registered representatives) are permitted to perform various functions within their firm. These roles will largely be based off the qualifying exams the individual has completed (there are different licensing exams for principals, investment bankers, municipal securities dealers, etc.) A non-registered person is simply an individual who does not meet these criteria. When an individual is taking the SIE and FINRA licensing exams (even when sponsored by a FINRA member firm) they are considered to be unregistered. Once all applicable exams are complete and the Form U4 has been satisfactorily completed, an individual can be registered by the firm.

PERMITTED ACTIVITIES OF REGISTERED AND NON-REGISTERED PERSONS

Registered persons can execute their full responsibilities within the firm. These can include making recommendations on behalf of the broker-dealer as well as soliciting orders from clients. The tasks will vary based off the associated person's qualifying exams, as well as role responsibilities. A non-registered person is only allowed to perform tasks that are clerical or administrative in nature. For example, a non-registered person can file paperwork, carry out tasks assigned by their managers, or assist with other administrative duties. It is prohibited for a non-registered person to solicit orders or make recommendations on behalf of the broker-dealer. If the task is clerical or administrative in nature, it's a non-registered person; if it's not, then it's the responsibility of an appropriately-licensed registered person.

INELIGIBILITY FOR MEMBERSHIP OR ASSOCIATION

Since the securities industry is highly regulated, there are very specific rules and regulations that firms must follow when hiring new talent. In addition, there are explicitly stated requirements for association with a firm, as well as disqualifying elements. Disqualifying elements that would lead to ineligibility for membership include securities related misdemeanors, felony convictions in the previous 10 years, injunctions by a court related to securities dealings, bars by the SEC, denial of registration with FINRA or a member firm, association with certain disqualified persons, etc. The full list of disqualifying events is included in Section 3(a)(39) of the Exchange Act. If a person is not a member of a firm and is not registered, then they cannot conduct securities dealings legally.

BACKGROUND CHECKS

Since the registered individuals in the securities industry have a very important role, FINRA wishes to ensure that only qualified individuals hold those positions. A background check is required to register with FINRA. When a firm hires an individual, the offer is contingent on satisfactory completion of a background check. This allows the member firm and FINRA to determine if the individual is qualified. According to the letter of the law, the firm has a wide berth in terms of the thoroughness of the background check. The investigate the person's character, business reputation, experience, and qualifications. Firms spend a significant amount of money on licensing and onboarding for new associates, so it is in their best interested to catch any disqualifying activities or elements as early as possible.

FINGERPRINTING

In line with the extensive background check element of registration with FINRA, prospective members are required to submit fingerprints to their employing BD. These fingerprints go through Electronic Fingerprint Processing (EFP) which allows FINRA to share information with the FBI. FINRA is able to check an individual's background for any potential disqualifying elements. Registration with FINRA and a member firm is contingent on successful completion of fingerprinting, similar to the background check process.

FAILING TO REGISTER AN ASSOCIATED PERSON

All registered representatives must be registered with FINRA (or the necessary SRO), in addition to the firm. Failure to appropriately register the individual could lead to disciplinary action. This would affect both the firm and the individual. In addition, the firm is required to notify FINRA no later than 30 calendar days after the fact whenever a change has taken place with the association of a member. Events that would be reportable include discovering that the member is in violation of securities law, written customer complaints filed against the member, denial of registration, involvement with a disqualified member, and legal proceedings (among others).

When an individual seeks registration with a FINRA member firm, they must pass a background check as well as submit fingerprints. There are various things that can serve as statutory disqualifications for registration. These include but are not limited to any felony convictions within the last ten years, misdemeanors involving securities or monies, and previous denial, suspension, or revocation of registration with FINRA. These prohibitions exist to bar people with a criminal history (namely, securities-related crime) from registering or re-registering with FINRA. It is unlikely that someone who is suspended or had their registration revoked in the past will ever be able to attain it again.

STATE REGISTRATION REQUIREMENTS

BDs are required by FINRA and NASAA to register with the state administrator for any state in which they do business. This means if a BD has an employee, office, or customer in a state, they must be registered with that state. This is where blue-sky laws come into effect, as there are particular rules from state to state regarding the sale of certain securities and annuities. For example, to sell insurance products in a state the associated person is required to obtain state insurance licenses, whether they be for health, life or another form of insurance. This goes back to the layered structure of regulation between the state and federal governments. It is essential that firms register with any state in which they do business. The Series 63, 65, and 66 are all NASAA exams delivered by FINRA that members must take after the general 6 or 7 exams.

CONTINUING EDUCATION (CE) REQUIREMENT

Firms will set specific continuing education requirements for their members. This ensures that members do not lose their edge. Remember that if a member is separated from a firm and the industry, they have two years to re-register or their licenses will expire and they must retest. It is similar with continuing education. FINRA sets a baseline regulatory requirement for continuing education. FINRA requires continuing education within 120 days after your two-year anniversary, and then every three years thereafter. A firm can add additional requirements on top of this, but FINRA sets the minimum that must be followed to be in compliance.

Employee Conduct and Reportable Events

EMPLOYEE CONDUCT

FORM U4 AND FORM U5

Simply put, the Form U4 is "hello" and the Form U5 is "goodbye." The Form U4 is what individuals fill out when joining a FINRA member firm. It is then filed by the company. The Form U5 is filled when an employee leaves a firm for any reason. With the Form U4, individuals are asked a variety of questions that link with the potential statutory disqualifications. Any "yes" answers on Form U4 are not a good thing. It is prohibited to file misleading information on either form, just as it is prohibited to omit information. Amendments to forms must be made within thirty days, and any individual that leaves the security industry must reaffiliate within two years or have to retest. The "parking of registration" is where an individual seeks to stay listed as a registered member for as long as possible to avoid the start of the two-year clock; this is prohibited. These forms must be updated whenever a change in the status of the member occurs. For instance, if a member becomes involved in a court case relating to securities fraud, FINRA must be notified.

CUSTOMER COMPLAINTS

Any and all customer complaints must be handled by a supervisor in the firm. This means that an individual cannot file customer complaints that have to do with themselves. The firm is required to file these customer complaints with FINRA on a quarterly basis. This is to ensure transparency and fairness, which are very important for the effective operations of firms in the securities industry. In addition, a complaint only refers to written communication. A verbal complaint does not constitute a complaint that must be brought to the attention of the principal. So, associated persons will ensure to get the complaint in writing so that it can be appropriately filed.

POTENTIAL RED FLAGS

Red flags from a customer would include suspicious activities, actions inconsistent with prior behavior, behavior that does not fall within the scope of the "prudent man" framework, etc. RRs should be acutely aware of any behavior that could be indicative of money laundering, fraud, or otherwise illegal activities. These must be reported up the chain. On RR side, potential red flags include but are not limited to guaranteeing investment performance, acting in a manner that is not in accordance with firm or FINRA policies, churning a customer's account to generate extra commissions or fees, and any actions that are not in the best interest of the customer. Regulatory oversight is essential to avoid potential lawsuits and ensure good faith on the part of both the customer and the associated person.

REPORTABLE EVENTS

OUTSIDE BUSINESS ACTIVITIES

Outside business activities are activities that registered persons engage in that are outside the scope of their role with the member firm and are done to receive payment. Usually, individuals will be barred or restricted from engaging in OBAs that could create a conflict of interest with their role in the firm. An example of this would be restricting a financial advisor at one firm from offering their services to clients outside of the business for personal pay. Other reportable business activities include serving on a board of a company or a part-time job at a local business (even if it is not in the realm of financial services). Registered members are required to submit written notice of any OBAs with their employing broker-dealer whenever they take on an OBA with probable cause of payment. It is up to the firm is to whether they will limit or restrict these activities in accordance with FINRA and firm guidelines.

PRIVATE SECURITIES TRANSACTIONS

Registered representatives are prohibited from selling clients products that are not on the firm's approved product list. This is referred to as "selling away". Not all PSTs are illegal, but a firm must note these transactions and file them as if they were done through the firm like a normal transaction. Prior to a PST, the associated person must provide written notice to their firm describing the transaction and any pertinent information. This can include transactions that are done for pay as well as those that are done without pay.

REPORTING OF POLITICAL CONTRIBUTIONS AND CONSEQUENCES FOR EXCEEDING DOLLAR CONTRIBUTION THRESHOLDS

According to MSRB G-37 (Municipal Securities Rulemaking Board General rule 37), registered representatives can donate no more than $250 per election cycle for a politician the RR can vote for. The reason for this is to avoid a conflict of interest where an associated person or firm donates large sums of money to a municipal government official in order to receive preferable treatment in the future. This usually takes the form of underwriting business for municipal bonds. If the politician is not elected, there is no limit on funds that can be donated as "cleaning up" costs associated with the campaign. Violation of these rules can lead to a ban on business with the municipality, usually for two years.

DOLLAR AND VALUE LIMITS FOR GIFTS AND GRATUITIES AND NON-CASH COMPENSATION

There is a set limit of $100 for gifts and non-cash compensation both to and from an RR. This means an associated person cannot accept gifts in excess of $100, nor can they give gifts to clients in excess of $100. This is to avoid conflicts of interest. This applies to non-cash compensation as well. RRs cannot accept deals that would be illegal or not in the best interest of the firm. Business entertainment has no limit and usually includes activities like client dinners. The associated person is required to submit notice in writing of these activities to their firm in order to ensure compliance and transparency.

FELONY, FINANCIAL-RELATED MISDEMEANORS, LIENS, BANKRUPTCY

As with most things, any time there is a change to an employee's Form U4 FINRA must be notified. Of course, the employee must also make the firm aware of any changes in their status that could affect their role. Examples of activities that must be reported include felony accusations, acquittals or convictions; securities-related misdemeanors; liens; and/or bankruptcy. These would all affect an associated person and usually lead to disqualification and separation from the industry. FINRA takes these rules very seriously in order to ensure safety for investors.

SIE Practice Test #1

Want to take this practice test in an online interactive format?
Check out the bonus page, which includes interactive practice questions and
much more: **mometrix.com/bonus948/seriessie**

1. A registered principal or registered representative must retake the qualifying exam if his or her registration has been revoked or terminated for a period of _____ or more.

   a. 1 year
   b. 2 years
   c. 3 years
   d. 5 years

2. An options contract that gives the holder the right to purchase the number of shares of the underlying security is a _____.

   a. Put
   b. Covered
   c. Uncovered
   d. Call

3. What are the three General Telemarketing Requirements as stated in FINRA Rule 3230?

   a. Time of Day Restriction, State Do-Not-Call List, and National Do-Not-Call List
   b. State Do-Not-Call List, National Do-Not-Call List, and Firm-Specific Do-Not-Call List
   c. Time of Day Restriction, Firm-Specific Do-Not-Call List, and State Do-Not Call List
   d. Time of Day Restriction, National Do-Not-Call List, and Firm-Specific Do Not Call List

4. Excessive trading in a customer's account for no apparent reason other than to generate commissions is _____.

   a. Churning
   b. Rebalancing
   c. Market-timing
   d. Front-running

5. Which of the following is not a prohibited activity?

   a. Rebalancing
   b. Commingling funds
   c. Guarantees against loss
   d. Spreading market rumors

6. Any material for use in any newspaper, magazine, or other public medium, or by radio, television, or telephone recording, is referred to as _____.

   a. An advertisement
   b. A market letter
   c. A research report
   d. Sales literature

7. What is the minimum time period that may be used in material promoting past records of research recommendations in connection with purchases or sales?

   a. Six months
   b. One year
   c. Three years
   d. Five years

8. Annual continuing education training provided by member firms is known as_____.

   a. Firm Continuing Education
   b. Compliance Training
   c. Firm Element Training
   d. Firm Regulatory Training

9. Which of the following items does not need to be reported on Form U4?

   a. Bankruptcy
   b. DUI
   c. Medical condition
   d. Address change

10. Which of the following statements are true with respect to options communications that include historical performance?

   a. A Registered Options Principal determines that the records or statistics fairly present the status of the recommendations or transactions reported upon
   b. All relevant costs, including commissions, fees, and daily margin obligations, are disclosed and reflected in the performance
   c. They must state that the results presented should not and cannot be viewed as an indicator of future performance
   d. All of the above

11. Which of the following is false regarding collateralized mortgage obligation (CMO) advertisements?

   a. Advertisements may not contain a comparison with any other investment vehicle.
   b. Advertisements may contain comparisons with CDs.
   c. Advertisements must include a description of the initial issue tranche.
   d. Advertisements that contain an anticipated yield must disclose the prepayment assumption used to calculate the yield.

12. Which of the following items are required in a research report that contains ratings?

   a. The meaning of each rating must be defined.
   b. The percentage of all securities rated by the member to which the member would assign a "buy," "hold/neutral," or "sell" rating must be disclosed.
   c. The member must disclose the percentage of subject companies within the "buy," "hold/neutral," and "sell" ratings for whom the member has provided investment banking services within the previous 12 months.
   d. All of the above.

13. Which of the following written communications is considered a research report?

a. An email that includes an analysis of equity securities of individual companies
b. A discussion of broad-based indices
c. A commentary on economic, political, or market conditions
d. A technical analysis concerning the demand and supply for a sector, index, or industry based on trading volume and price

14. What is the limit of SIPC protection if a brokerage firm fails?

a. $100,000
b. $250,000
c. $500,000
d. $1,000,000

15. If a person has made lifetime gifts totaling $4,000,000 and dies in 2023, what is the amount that will be paid in taxes if the total remaining estate is $20,000,000?

a. $2,481,000
b. $4,377,800
c. $4,432,000
d. $4,968,000

16. What is the cost basis of securities received as an inheritance?

a. The current market price at the time the securities are received by the heir
b. The purchase price of the securities when they were originally bought
c. The market price on the date of death
d. The market price on the date of the original purchase

17. Which of the following securities are exempt from registration under the Securities Act of 1933?

a. Common stock
b. Municipal bond
c. Corporate bond
d. Preferred stock

18. ________ has the power to register, regulate, and oversee brokerage firms, transfer agents, and clearing agencies as well as SROs.

a. NASD
b. FINRA
c. SEC
d. MSRB

19. Which of the following item(s) can affect an investor's risk tolerance?

a. Age
b. Time frame
c. Personal experience
d. All of the above

20. Which of the following investments would not be considered appropriate for an investor with an objective of current income?

a. Growth stock
b. Municipal bond
c. Corporate bond
d. Utility stock

21. What is the tax advantage of owning municipal bonds?

a. No federal taxes
b. No state taxes regardless of your state of residence
c. No state taxes if the municipality is in your state of residence
d. Both A and C

22. _____ is the process of buying investment vehicles that have a high degree of uncertainty regarding their future value and expected earnings.

a. Speculation
b. Hedging
c. Gambling
d. Risk aversion

23. Which of the following scenarios would be considered an unsuitable recommendation?

a. Recommending a CD purchase to an elderly risk-averse investor
b. Recommending a common stock to a 30-year-old with a growth objective
c. Recommending a speculative stock to a recently retired investor who is risk averse
d. Recommending a growth stock mutual fund to a 30-year-old investor with a growth objective

24. If a registered representative receives a customer complaint, what should he or she do first?

a. Try to handle the customer by himself or herself
b. Notify the branch manager or designated compliance individual
c. Notify the Chief Compliance Officer of the broker-dealer
d. Nothing

25. Which of the following investments would be most suitable for a young investor who can only invest a small amount each month?

a. Common stock
b. Corporate bond
c. Options
d. Mutual fund

26. A corporate bond would be least suitable for which of the following investors?

a. A 25-year-old interested in speculative investments
b. A 25-year-old with an investment objective of growth and income
c. A retired individual with an investment objective of growth and income
d. A retired individual with an investment objective of income

27. In a community property state, how are assets divided between a husband and wife in a divorce?

 a. 100% belongs to the husband
 b. 100% belongs to the wife
 c. 50% belong to the husband and 50% belong to the wife
 d. 100% of the assets must remain jointly owned

28. Which of the following documents may be used to give a third party trading authorization on an account?

 a. POA
 b. TOD
 c. Stock power
 d. Account agreement

29. Which of the following information is not required as part of the requirement to know your customer?

 a. Occupation and employer
 b. Investment experience
 c. Legal address
 d. Level of education

30. In response to which event was the USA PATRIOT Act created?

 a. The attack on Pearl Harbor on December 7, 1941
 b. The bombing of the World Trade Center on February 26, 1993
 c. The attack on the World Trade Center on September 11, 2001
 d. The bombing of the Boston Marathon on April 15, 2013

31. All of the following are true regarding a suspicious activity report (SAR) except:

 a. The deadline to file a SAR is 30 calendar days after becoming aware of any suspicious transaction or pattern of suspicious transactions or activities.
 b. You are protected from civil liability when you report suspicious activity.
 c. You are only required to file a SAR if you believe the activity is suspicious and involves $2,000 or more.
 d. You must tell the person involved in the transaction that a SAR has been filed.

32. A type of mutual fund or exchange-traded fund (ETF) whose investment objective is to achieve approximately the same return as a specific market index, such as the S&P 500, is called a(n) _____.

 a. Value fund
 b. Index fund
 c. Balanced fund
 d. Growth fund

33. Unsystematic risk is also known as _____.

 a. Market risk
 b. Purchasing power risk
 c. Credit risk
 d. Diversifiable risk

34. The risk that a security will be redeemed prior to its maturity date is known as _____.

    a. Market risk
    b. Call risk
    c. Event risk
    d. Systematic risk

35. What type of bonds are high-risk securities that have received low ratings and produce high yields?

    a. Junk bonds
    b. Municipal bonds
    c. Junior bonds
    d. Convertible bonds

36. What is another name for an unrealized gain?

    a. Paper profit
    b. Capital gain
    c. Capital loss
    d. Hypothetical gain

37. If a company declares a 3:2 stock split, how many additional shares will an investor with 200 shares receive?

    a. 100 shares
    b. 200 shares
    c. 400 shares
    d. 600 shares

38. When interest rates increase, what happens to bond prices?

    a. Bond prices increase
    b. Bond prices decrease
    c. Bond prices may increase or decrease
    d. Changes in interest rate have no effect on bond prices

39. An option to buy shares of a new issue of common stock at a specified price, over a specified, fairly short period of time, is a _____.

    a. Right
    b. Warrant
    c. Call
    d. Put

40. Which of the following statements is false regarding short selling?

    a. Money is made when prices fall.
    b. Short selling carries high risk and a limited return.
    c. Short selling carries low risk and an unlimited return.
    d. Money is lost when prices rise.

41. What is the dividend amount that a shareholder who owns 100 shares will receive in the following scenario?

> ABC Corporation declared a $0.25 dividend to shareholders of record on Monday, December 5, payable on December 15. The closing price of ABC Corporation stock on December 5 is $20.34.

    a. $0.25
    b. $2.50
    c. $25.00
    d. $250.00

42. Which of the following types of stocks are considered defensive stocks?

    a. Public utilities
    b. Gold mining
    c. Technology companies
    d. Both A and B

43. What is the tax rate on a long-term capital gain for an individual in the highest income tax bracket?

    a. 10%
    b. 15%
    c. 20%
    d. 25%

44. _____ represents the debts of a company.

    a. Assets
    b. Liabilities
    c. Equity
    d. Cash flow

45. Which financial statement provides a financial summary of the operating results of the company?

    a. Income statement
    b. Balance sheet
    c. Cash flow statement
    d. Annual report

46. _____ are municipal bonds backed by the revenue-generating capacity of the issuer.

    a. Revenue bonds
    b. General obligation bonds
    c. Agency bonds
    d. Treasury notes

47. Which of the following statements is true regarding a downward-sloping yield curve?

    a. It indicates that yields tend to increase with longer maturities.
    b. It indicates that rates for short- and long-term loans are essentially the same.
    c. It indicates that intermediate term rates are the highest.
    d. It indicates that short-term rates are higher than long-term rates.

48. If interest rates are expected to rise in the near future, which of the following statements is true regarding duration?

    a. A longer duration would be preferred.
    b. A shorter duration would be preferred.
    c. There would be no preference regarding duration.
    d. A mid-term duration would be preferred.

Use the following information to answer the next two questions.

Net profit after taxes:	$18,000	Stockholder's Equity:	$170,000
Total revenues:	$615,000	Preferred dividends:	$5,000
Total assets:	$340,000	Number of common shares outstanding:	3,800
Current assets:	$280,000	Current liabilities:	$85,000
Earnings per share:	$4.75	Market price:	$49.50

49. What is the net profit margin?

    a. 10.59%
    b. 10.42%
    c. 2.92%
    d. 3.29%

50. What is the P/E ratio?

    a. 10.42
    b. 10.59
    c. 5.29
    d. 3.29

51. What rating must a bond receive to be considered investment grade?

    a. Aaa/AAA
    b. Aa/AA
    c. A/A
    d. Baa/BBB

52. An order to buy a stock at specific price or better is what type of order?

    a. Limit order
    b. Stop order
    c. Market order
    d. Stop limit order

53. A stop limit order to sell 100 shares of ABC Corporation (ABC) stock at $35 is entered when the current market price of ABC stock is $45. The company announces lower-than-expected earnings and the stock price falls dramatically. Under which of the following scenarios will the order not execute?

    a. The market price immediately falls to $35 and then rebounds to trade between $35 and $36 before falling below $35 again.
    b. The market price immediately falls to $35 and continues to fall without rebounding.
    c. The market price immediately falls to $35 and continues to trade between $33 and $36.
    d. The market price immediately falls to $35 and continues to trade between $35 and $37.

54. How often must customers receive account statements from a brokerage firm?
   a. Monthly, regardless of activity
   b. Monthly, if activity, otherwise semiannually
   c. Monthly, if activity, otherwise quarterly
   d. Quarterly, regardless of activity

55. If an option expires without hitting its strike price, what happens to the buyer and seller?
   a. The seller keeps the premium received and the buyer loses the premium paid.
   b. The seller keeps the premium received and loses the shares of the underlying security.
   c. The buyer loses the premium paid, but receives the shares of the underlying security.
   d. Nothing happens.

56. What is the amount of the "catch-up" contribution to a traditional or Roth IRA that individuals aged 50 and over may make in 2023?
   a. $500
   b. $1,000
   c. $1,500
   d. $2,000

57. What is the tax consequence to an individual under the age of 59 ½ who withdraws a lump sum from his 401(k)?
   a. The amount withdrawn is considered income and is subject to income taxes at the individual's rate.
   b. The amount that is withdrawn is considered income and is subject to income taxes at the individual's current rate. Plus, he may be subject to a 10% penalty.
   c. He must pay a 10% penalty. Otherwise, there are no tax consequences.
   d. None of the above. A lump sum withdrawal from a 401(k) is not a taxable event.

58. Contributions made to a traditional or Roth IRA may consist of _____.
   a. Cash only
   b. Cash or securities
   c. Cash, securities, or fine arts
   d. Securities only

59. What are the tax consequences to an individual who converts a traditional IRA into a Roth IRA?
   a. There are no tax consequences.
   b. The amount converted is taxed as income at a flat rate of 15%.
   c. The amount converted is taxed as income at a flat rate of 25%.
   d. The amount converted is taxed as income at the individual's current tax rate.

60. What is the current yield of a 5% bond that is priced at 80?
   a. 5.00%
   b. 6.25%
   c. 4.00%
   d. 8.00%

61. What is the buying power in a margin account?

   a. The amount of available cash
   b. The amount of margin available to borrow
   c. The amount of available cash plus the amount able to be borrowed
   d. None of the above. Margin accounts do not have buying power.

62. If an investor writes a covered call and wishes to close the transaction, he needs to enter which of the following trades:

   a. Sell to close
   b. Buy to close
   c. Sell to open
   d. Both A and B

63. All of the following are true of an investor's rights in a rights offering except that

   a. in the event the investor chooses to not purchase the shares offered, he or she may sell those rights to another investor.
   b. the investor chooses to purchase the shares.
   c. the investor's rights expire after 35 days due to the current market price dropping below the offering's subscription price.
   d. all of the above are true.

64. Which of the following describe characteristics of a shareholder's preemptive rights?

   a. In the event that the number of new shares proposed to be sold by the corporation causes the number of outstanding shares to outnumber the number of shares they are authorized to sell, the current shareholders must approve the increase to authorized shares before the sale can proceed.
   b. Current shareholders are given the first option to purchase any new shares sold by a corporation.
   c. Only after current shareholders have declined the offer to purchase shares from the corporation's new offering can the shares be offered for sale to the general investing public.
   d. All of the above are true.

65. Which of the following terms can be described as the day the decision is made by the corporation's board of directors to provide the common stockholders with a dividend?

   a. Declaration date
   b. Record date
   c. Ex-dividend date
   d. None of the above

66. What are some characteristics of preferred stock?

   a. Unless noted differently, par value for these shares is $1,000.
   b. Ownership of these shares provides a means of fixed income for an investor through dividend payments.
   c. Due to the fixed income nature of these shares, changes in interest rates have no effect on the price of these shares.
   d. Maturity dates for these shares range from 1 to 25 years.

67. All of the following are true of the transferability of securities except that

    a. securities can be transferred between parties by physically exchanging stock certificates.

    b. a stock owner does not need the approval of the issuing organization of that stock to sell his or her shares.

    c. the secondary market is where the transferring of securities is executed.

    d. a broker dealer may assist in the transferring process of securities between two parties.

68. Of the different types of preferred stock, which one has the feature of enabling its owner to receive both the preferred and common dividend?

    a. Cumulative preferred

    b. Callable preferred

    c. Participating preferred

    d. Convertible preferred

69. Of the following, which is the LEAST likely to be utilized by economists in analyzing the overall condition of the economy?

    a. Oil prices

    b. Supply and demand

    c. Gross domestic product (GDP)

    d. Fluctuations in the country's business cycle

70. The stock market will be negatively impacted by all of the following except

    a. an increase in taxation.

    b. a money supply reduction.

    c. an interest rate reduction.

    d. reduced government spending.

71. When considering the four stages of an economic business cycle, which of the following are characteristics of the expansion stage?

    I. Decline in savings
    II. Real estate prices on the rise
    III. An increase in gross domestic product (GDP)
    IV. Rise in inventories

    a. II, III, and IV

    b. III only

    c. II and III

    d. I, II, and III

72. Which of the following is an example of a company in the defensive sector?

    a. Manufacturing

    b. Automobile

    c. Computer

    d. Pharmaceutical

73. What does a buy limit order do?

    a. Allows an investor to set a maximum price he or she is willing to pay for a security

    b. Allows an investor to set a minimum price at which he or she is willing to sell a security

    c. Guarantees execution

    d. All of the above

74. **A specialist can handle all of the following types of orders except for**
    a. stop orders.
    b. market orders.
    c. AON orders.
    d. buy limit orders.

75. **What does security arbitrage involve?**
    a. Simultaneously buying and selling both a stock and a security that may be converted into that same underlying stock
    b. Buying shares in a company that is being taken over or acquired while shorting shares in the company about to acquire them
    c. Simultaneously buying and selling the same security in two different markets to exploit the price difference between the two
    d. None of the above

Answer Key and Explanations for Test #1

1. B: A person whose registration has been terminated or revoked for a period of more than two years must retake the qualifying exam. A person must retake the SIE exam as well if a period of more than four years has elapsed.

2. D: A call is an option contract that gives the holder the right to purchase the number of shares of the underlying security. A put is an option contract that gives the holder the right to sell the number of shares of the underlying security. A covered option means that the option writer's obligation is secured by a specific deposit whereas an uncovered option means that the option writer's obligation is not secured.

3. D: The three General Telemarketing Requirements are the Time of Day Restriction, the Firm-Specific Do-Not-Call List and the National Do-Not-Call List.

4. A: Churning is excessive trading in a customer's account for no reason other than to generate commissions. Rebalancing refers to adjusting a customer's portfolio to return to previously set ratios of investment types. Market-timing is the practice of timing or calculating the market's low and high points, buying when it is low and selling when it is high. Front-running is an unethical, and generally illegal, activity in which a broker makes advantageous trades by using non-public information about an impending transaction.

5. A: Rebalancing is not a prohibited activity, while commingling funds, guaranteeing against loss, and spreading market rumors are prohibited.

6. A: The term advertisement refers to any material for use in any newspaper, magazine, or other public medium, or by radio, television, or telephone recording. A market letter, sometimes referred to as an investment newsletter, is a paid publication that focuses on a particular segment or type investments. A research report is typically a private report prepared for by an investment bank's research team for use by their customers. Sales literature is written material that outlines a product and its benefits, typically produced by the entity that is selling the product. Sales literature is often required to have a disclaimer noting the risks associated with investing.

7. B: Material promoting past records of research recommendations, in connection with purchases or sales, must cover at least a one-year time period.

8. C: The annual continuing education training provided by member firms is known as Firm Element Training. Firm Continuing Education and Firm Regulatory Training are not the correct terms for FINRA continuing education. Compliance Training is a general term for employee training mandated by legislation, regulation, or policy; it is not specific to Series license holders.

9. C: Medical conditions do not need to be reported on Form U4. A bankruptcy filing, DUI, and address change must be reported promptly on the registered representative's Form U4.

10. D: All of the statements are true with respect to options communications that include historical performance.

11. B: CMO advertisements may not contain comparisons with any other investment vehicle, including CDs.

12. D: A research report that contains ratings must define the meaning of each rating; the percentage of all securities rated by the member to which the member would assign a "buy," "hold/neutral," or "sell" rating must be disclosed; and the member must disclose the percentage of subject companies within the "buy," "hold/neutral," and "sell" ratings for whom the member has provided investment banking services within the previous 12 months.

13. A: An email that includes an analysis of equity securities of individual companies is considered a research report. Discussions of broad-based indices, commentaries on economic, political, or market conditions, and a technical analysis concerning the demand and supply for a sector, index, or industry based on trading volume and price are specifically excluded from the definition of a research report.

14. C: SIPC protects the securities and cash in a brokerage account up to $500,000 if a brokerage firm fails. The $500,000 protection includes up to $250,000 in cash in the brokerage account.

15. B: If a person has made lifetime gifts totaling $4,000,000 and dies in 2023, the amount that will be paid in taxes if the total remaining estate is $20,000,000 is $4,776,000. ($12,920,000 - $4,000,000 = $8,920,000 remaining exclusion amount; $20,000,000 - $8,920,000 = $11,080,000 taxable amount; $345,800 + $10,080,000 x 40% = $4,377,800.)

16. C: The cost basis of securities received as an inheritance is the market price on the date of death.

17. B: A municipal bond is exempt from registration, under the Securities Act of 1933, because it is issued by a government agency. Common stock, preferred stock, and corporate bonds are required to be registered because they are not issued by entities with high credit standing or by government agencies.

18. C: The SEC has the power to register, regulate, and oversee brokerage firms, transfer agents, and clearing agencies as well as SROs. The National Association of Securities Dealers (NASD), which existed from 1939 to 2007, oversaw the securities industry prior to the formation of FINRA. The Municipal Securities Rulemaking Board (MSRB) protects investors, issuers, and public pension plans by promoting a fair and efficient municipal market. The non-governmental agency known as FINRA (Financial Industry Regulatory Authority) governs registered agents and firms in the United States.

19. D: Age, time frame, and personal experience can all affect an investor's risk tolerance.

20. A: A growth stock would not be considered appropriate for an investor with an objective of current income. Older investors, or those who are looking for more conservative securities, prefer value stocks that pay dividends, CDs with predetermined interest and consistent payouts, or bonds that pay interest and cannot lose value. Younger investors would prefer growth, or aggressive, stocks because of the potential short-term gain if the stocks do well, since they have time to recover the invested amount if the stocks do poorly.

21. D: The tax advantage of owning municipal bonds is that they are not subject to federal taxes and also avoid state taxes if the municipality is in the investor's state of residence.

22. A: Speculation is the process of buying investment vehicles that have a high degree of uncertainty regarding their future value and expected earnings. Hedging is an investment strategy that seeks to reduce the impact of negative movements in price of a security. Gambling is fundamentally different from investing in that it relies entirely on chance. Risk-averse, or conservative, investors are those who are willing to settle for lower rates of return on their investments in exchange for a lower risk of losing the principal they have invested.

23. C: Recommending a speculative stock to a recently retired investor who is risk averse would be considered an unsuitable recommendation. Speculative, aggressive, or growth stocks would not be a good fit for older or retired investors that are risk averse. Older investors tend to be more conservative and are looking for stable income. Both common stocks and growth stock mutual funds are perfectly within a younger investor's goal for growth.

24. B: If a registered representative (RR) receives a customer complaint, the first thing he or she should do is notify the branch manager or designated compliance individual. FINRA Rule 4513 states that customer complaints must be submitted in writing and kept for at least four years on record. Complaints must be reported by the 15th day of the month.

25. D: A mutual fund would be the most suitable investment for a young investor who can only invest a small amount each month. Investing in the S&P 500 Index Fund would allow newer, younger investors to enjoy the outstanding performance of multiple companies without requiring outstanding investment knowledge or experience. Assuming that the young investor has little capital to invest in stocks and maintain a diversified portfolio, common stocks might leave the investor at a loss if other stocks perform better. Corporate bonds are better suited for conservative investors who are more concerned about steady income, as well as avoiding the risk of losing their initial investment. Options may be too complex for young investors who have no prior experience. Investing in options without proper knowledge could lead to overleveraging and speculation.

26. A: A corporate bond would be least suitable for a 25-year-old interested in speculative investments. Again, corporate bonds, and bonds in general, are better suited for conservative investors who are seeking steady, predetermined income.

27. C: In a community property state, when a husband and wife divorce, the assets are divided so that 50% belong to the husband and 50% belong to the wife.

28. A: A POA (power of attorney) document may be used to give trading authorization on an account to a third party.

29. D: A customer's level of education is not required as part of the requirement to know your customer (KYC).

30. C: The USA PATRIOT Act was enacted after the attack on the World Trade Center on September 11, 2001.

31. D: It is illegal to tell the person involved in the transaction that a SAR has been filed. The other three statements are true. The deadline to file a SAR is 30 calendar days after becoming aware of any suspicious transaction or pattern of suspicious transactions or activities. You are protected from civil liability when you report suspicious activity. You are only required to file a SAR if you believe the activity is suspicious and involves $2,000 or more.

32. B: A type of mutual fund or ETF whose investment objective is to achieve approximately the same return as a specific market index, such as the S&P 500, is called an index fund.

33. D: Unsystematic risk is also known as diversifiable risk. It results from random events such as labor strikes or lawsuits and affects various investment vehicles differently. It is this type of risk that can be eliminated through diversification.

34. B: The risk that a security will be redeemed prior to its maturity date is known as call risk. Market risk is the potential for loss due to the performance of the financial market. Event risk is the risk of an unexpected event negatively affecting an investment's value. Systematic risk is essentially the same as market risk.

35. A: Junk bonds (also called high yield bonds) are high-risk securities that have received low ratings and produce high yields. Municipal bonds are tax-exempt, so investors do not have to pay taxes on the interest from the bonds. A junior bond is corporate debt that, in the event of bankruptcy, will be repaid only after all other debts have been repaid. A convertible bond is a corporate bond that may be exchanged for stock in the company at maturity in lieu of receiving the face value as cash.

36. A: Paper profit is another name for an unrealized gain. If it was an unrealized loss, it would be called paper loss. A capital gain is a realized gain and a capital loss is a realized loss. Hypothetical gain is not a real term.

37. A: If a company declares a 3:2 stock split, an investor with 200 shares will receive an additional 100 shares of stock.

38. B: When interest rates increase, bond prices decrease. Bonds have an inverse relationship to interest rates. Most bonds pay a fixed interest rate that becomes more attractive if interest rates fall as there will be more investor demand that will drive up the price of the bond. Conversely, if interest rates rise, investors will no longer prefer the lower fixed interest rate paid by a bond, resulting in a decline in the price of the bond.

39. A: A right, as pertaining to a rights offering, is an option to buy one or more shares of common stock in a given company when new shares are issued, at a price initially below the market price, within a short timeframe, usually a month or less. A warrant is an option issued by a given company to buy one or more shares of common stock in that company at a price initially *above* the market price. Warrants are typically valid for multiple years. An option with the right to buy is known as a call option, and an option with the right to sell is known as a put option. Calls and puts are contracts made between participants in the marketplace rather than issued by a company.

40. C: Short selling does not carry low risk and an unlimited return. Short selling makes money when prices fall, it carries high risk, and it has a limited return. Short selling loses money when prices rise.

41. C: A shareholder who owns 100 shares will receive $25.00 (100 × 0.25). The price of the stock does not affect the dividend payout. Dividends are usually declared quarterly, though some companies may do it annually. A dividend yield would be the sum of the quarterly payouts (e.g. $0.25 × 4 = $1) divided by the current price of the stock (e.g. 1/25.34 = 0.039 = 3.9%).

42. D: Both public utility and gold mining stocks are considered defensive stocks. Technology companies are considered aggressive or growth investments.

43. C: The maximum tax rate on a long-term capital gain is 20% for an individual in the highest tax bracket. Long-term capital gains are the net sales on assets held for more than one year. For TY 2023, the highest tax bracket begins at income levels of $492,300 (Single), $553,850 (Married Filing Jointly), or $276,900 (Married Filing Separately).

44. B: Liabilities represent the debts of a company. Assets are resources held by the company that have immediate value or that will provide a future benefit. Equity represents the amount of stockholders' capital in a firm. Cash flow is the amount of cash moving into and out of a company.

45. A: The income statement provides a financial summary of the operating results of the company. The balance sheet is a summary report of a company's assets and liabilities, along with stockholder equity. The cash flow statement provides a summary of a company's cash flow and other events that caused changes in their cash position. An annual report is a document describing operations and financial position that every company listed on the stock market must provide to its shareholders.

46. A: Revenue bonds are municipal bonds backed by the revenue-generating capacity of the issuer. Municipal bonds backed by the full faith and credit, and taxing power, of the issuer are called general obligation bonds. Agency bonds are issued by either an agency of the US government (other than the Treasury) or a government-sponsored enterprise (GSE) and may not be fully guaranteed. Treasury notes are bonds issued by the US Treasury and are backed by the full faith and credit of the US government.

47. D: An inverted, or downward-sloping, yield curve indicates that short-term rates are higher than long-term rates. A normal, upward-sloping yield curve indicates that yields tend to increase with longer maturities. A flat yield curve indicates that interest rates are similar across all available terms. A humped, or bell-shaped, curve indicates that medium-term (intermediate) rates are higher than either short- or long-term rates.

48. B: If interest rates are expected to rise in the near future, a shorter duration would be preferred. A longer duration would be preferred if interest rates are expected to fall.

49. C: The net profit margin is 2.92% (18,000/615,000).

50. A: The P/E ratio is 10.42 (49.50/4.75).

51. D: To be considered investment grade, a bond must receive a rating of at least Baa/BBB. Aaa/AAA and Aa/AA are the highest credit ratings, meaning these bonds are high quality investment grade. A/A is better than Baa/BBB, so these bonds are still investment grade.

52. A: An order to buy or sell a stock at a specific price or better is a limit order. A market order is an order to buy or sell at the best available price at the time the order is placed. A stop is an order to buy or sell a stock when its market price reaches or drops below a specified price. A stop limit order is an order to buy or sell at a specific price or better once a given stop price has been hit.

53. B: When the market price of ABC stock hits $35, the stop has been met and the order turns into a limit order to sell at $35 or higher. Since the market price continued to fall and stayed below $35, the limit order did not execute. In answers A, C, and D, the market price rose above the limit order price of $35. Therefore, those orders would execute.

54. C: Customers must receive account statements from brokerage firms at least every quarter. Often, firms will send monthly statements to account holders with any activity.

55. A: If an option expires without hitting its strike price, the seller keeps the premium received and the buyer loses the premium paid.

56. B: In TY 2023, the catch-up contribution to a traditional or Roth IRA that individuals aged 50 and over may make is $1,000, bringing the maximum total contribution amount for these individuals up to $7,500.

57. B: The tax consequence to an individual under the age of 59 ½ who withdraws a lump sum from a 401(k) is that the amount that is withdrawn is considered income and is subject to income taxes at the individual's current rate. The individual may also be subject to a 10% penalty for early withdrawal.

58. A: Contributions made to a traditional or Roth IRA may consist of cash only. Securities or fine arts may not be contributed to a traditional or Roth IRA. Any non-cash assets in a non-retirement brokerage account that are to be transferred to a retirement account, must first be liquidated (sold) so they can be transferred in as cash.

59. D: The tax consequences to an individual who converts a traditional IRA into a Roth IRA are that the amount converted is counted as income and is subject to the individual's current tax rate.

60. B: Bonds by default have a par value (also face value or nominal value) of $1,000, but bonds might trade for more or less, in which case they would be priced or quoted at some percentage of that. In this case, a bond that is priced at 80 would sell for $800. The percent tied to a bond is its coupon, and it is stated in terms of the par value. In this case, a bond with a 5% coupon, which can be called a 5% bond, would issue regular coupon payments of 5% of its par value, or $50.

Since the current yield of a bond refers to the actual interest income produced by that bond relative to the bond's market (not par) price, the current yield of a 5% bond priced at 80 would be $50 / $800 = 6.25%.

61. C: The buying power in a margin account is the amount of available cash plus the amount able to be borrowed. This is also called purchasing power.

62. D: If an investor has a covered call, this means that he has sold a call option to a third party and simultaneously has ownership of the underlying security for that option, e.g. selling a call option to purchase ABC stock while simultaneously owning (or buying) ABC stock. Accordingly, to close out this position, the investor would have to reverse both sides of this position, buying back the call option and selling the underlying security; this is then a combination of buying to close and selling to close.

63. C: Investors' rights expire only after 45 days. Additionally, investors may choose to exercise the rights to purchase additional shares or sell those rights to another investor who would like to buy those shares.

64. D: A shareholder's preemptive rights provide for him or her to receive the first option to purchase shares from any new offering conducted by the corporation, provide for the shares to be offered to the public only after they've been declined by the current shareholders, and require approval from the current shareholders for any increase to the number of the corporation's authorized shares.

65. A: The declaration date is the date when the board of directors declares the decision to pay out a dividend to common stockholders of record. The record date is when investors must be officially recorded as stockholders on stock certificates in order to qualify for receipt of the declared dividend. The ex-dividend date is the first day that the stock trades without the declared dividend attached and, accordingly, will not be given to anyone purchasing the stock as of this date or after.

66. B: Ownership in preferred stock provides a fixed income to the investor through dividend payments. The par value of shares is generally $100, not $1,000. Due to the fixed income nature of these shares, they are more sensitive to changes in interest rates, demonstrating an inverse relationship between rates and pricing. These shares have no maturity date and are therefore considered perpetual.

67. A: Securities are transferable only after the owner either endorses the stock certificates or signs a power of substitution into the new owner's name. Owners may sell shares without the approval of the requisite issuing organization, securities transfers are executed in the secondary market, and broker dealers assist in the securities transferring process.

68. C: Participating preferred stock ownership provides the investor the right to receive both the preferred and common dividend when paid. Cumulative preferred shares not only allow the owner payment of the preferred dividend but also provide protection against missed dividend payments by requiring back payment of those dividends. Callable shares afford the corporation the right to call in those shares, often at a premium price. Convertible shares allow for the option to exchange preferred shares for common shares at a conversion price.

69. A: In analyzing the overall condition of a country's economy, an economist would be least likely to utilize oil prices, and MORE likely to look to charts and models regarding supply and demand, the country's gross domestic product (GDP), and fluctuations in its business cycle.

70. C: Falling interest rates will have a positive effect on stock market performance. An increase in taxes, or a reduction in the money supply or government spending, will negatively impact the stock market.

71. C: With regards to the stages of an economic business cycle, the expansion stage would be characterized by a rise in real estate prices and an increase in gross domestic product (GDP). A decline in the amount and rate of savings and a rise in inventories would be characteristics of the contraction stage.

72. D: A pharmaceutical company would be categorized as defensive, providing products that are needed and will be purchased by individuals regardless of the state of the economy. Manufacturing and automobile companies would be cyclical, and a computer company would be growth.

73. A: A buy limit order allows protection to an investor by providing the chance to set a maximum price they are willing to pay for a security. A sell limit order allows an investor to set a minimum price at which he or she is willing to sell a security. A buy limit order provides price protection to the investor in that it guarantees he or she will not pay over a certain price for that security, but accordingly, it will NOT guarantee execution of that order in the event that the price level of that security does not reach the investor's desired price or below.

74. B: A specialist cannot accept market orders in that the nature of those types of orders dictates that they be executed as soon as they are presented to the market, and accordingly, there would be at that point no order to leave with the specialist.

75. A: Security arbitrage involves the simultaneous purchase and sale of both a stock and a security that may be converted into that same underlying stock. Buying shares in a company that is being taken over or acquired, while shorting shares in the company about to acquire them, is risk arbitrage. Simultaneously buying and selling the same security in two different markets in order to exploit the price difference between the two is market arbitrage.

SIE Practice Test #2

1. Within how many days must a member report to FINRA if the member or an associated person of the member is the subject of a written customer complaint involving allegations of theft or misappropriation of funds?

   a. 10 business days
   b. 15 calendar days
   c. 20 business days
   d. 30 calendar days

2. Correspondence means any written communication that is distributed to ____ or fewer retail investors within any ____-day period.

   a. 10 or fewer investors within any 10-day period
   b. 15 or fewer investors within any 20-day period
   c. 25 or fewer investors within any 30-day period
   d. 30 or fewer investors within any 25-day period

3. What is the dollar value that any gift from or to a member or person associated with a member may not exceed in one year?

   a. $0 (gifts are not allowed)
   b. $50
   c. $100
   d. $200

4. A registered representative trading an equity based on non-public information in his or her own account before trading for clients is called _____.

   a. Churning
   b. Rebalancing
   c. Market timing
   d. Front running

5. Which of the following items regarding SIPC must member firms advise all new customers of in writing when opening a new account?

   I. The SIPC website address
   II. The SIPC telephone number
   III. How to obtain the SIPC brochure

   a. I only
   b. I and III
   c. I and II
   d. I, II, and III

6. Which of the following terms refers to printed or processed analysis covering individual companies or industries?

   a. Advertisement
   b. Market letter
   c. Research report
   d. Sales literature

109

Copyright © Mometrix Media. You have been licensed one copy of this document for personal use only. Any other reproduction or redistribution is strictly prohibited. All rights reserved.
This content is provided for test preparation purposes only and does not imply an endorsement by Mometrix of any particular political, scientific, or religious point of view.

7. When using testimonials, which of the following points does not need to be clearly stated in the body copy of the material?

    a. The testimonial may not be representative of the experience of other clients.
    b. The fact that that it is a paid testimonial if a nominal sum is paid.
    c. If the testimonial concerns a technical aspect of investing, the person making the testimonial must have adequate knowledge and experience to form a valid opinion.
    d. The testimonial cannot be indicative of future performance or success.

8. Registered Investment Advisers are registered through the _____.

    a. FINRA
    b. SEC
    c. MSRB
    d. NYSE

9. Prior to the Options Disclosure Document (ODD) being delivered, a registered representative may do which of the following:

    a. Solicit a sale of an options contract as long as the ODD is sent before or at the time of sale
    b. Place an options trade for a client's account as long as the ODD is sent the same day
    c. Place an options trade for a client's account as long as the ODD is sent before settlement
    d. Limit discussions to general descriptions of the options

10. A municipal security advertisement that concerns the facilities, services, or skills with respect to municipal securities of such broker, dealer, or municipal securities dealer or of another broker, dealer, or municipal securities dealer is the definition of _____.

    a. Professional advertisement
    b. Product advertisement
    c. New issue product advertisement
    d. Municipal fund security product advertisement

11. A member may not publish a research report regarding a subject company for which the member acted as manager or co-manager of an IPO for _____ days following the date of the offering.

    a. 20 calendar days
    b. 20 business days
    c. 40 calendar days
    d. 40 business days

12. Which of the following is true regarding third-party research reports?

    a. A third-party research report is a research report produced by a person in the research department of a member firm.
    b. Third-party research reports and independent third-party research reports have the same meaning.
    c. A registered principal (or supervisory analyst) must approve all third-party research reports distributed by a member.
    d. A registered principal (or supervisory analyst) must approval all independent third-party research reports.

13. Which of the following accounts is not covered by FDIC?

a. Bank savings and checking accounts
b. Mutual fund account
c. Bank money market account
d. Certificates of deposit

14. What is the limit of FDIC protection per depositor, per insured bank, for each account ownership category?

a. $100,000
b. $250,000
c. $500,000
d. $1,000,000

15. What is the maximum amount that may be gifted within one calendar year (2023) to avoid taxation?

a. $14,000
b. $15,000
c. $16,000
d. $17,000

16. A _____ refers to when a company first sells it shares to the public.

a. Initial public offering
b. Initial marketing
c. Initial sales offering
d. Initial rights offering

17. The SEC was created under _____.

a. The Securities Act of 1933
b. The Securities Exchange Act of 1934
c. Investment Company Act of 1940
d. Investment Advisers Act of 1940

18. Which of the following financial information is not required on a new account application?

a. Net worth
b. Annual income
c. Liabilities
d. Liquid net worth

19. The length of time an investor plans to keep an investment is known as the _____.

a. Holding period
b. Time horizon
c. Quiet period
d. Calendar period

20. Which of the following investments would not be appropriate for an investor with a capital growth objective?

    a. Unit investment trust
    b. Common stock
    c. Growth mutual fund
    d. Zero coupon bond

21. Investing in multiple investment vehicles within a portfolio to reduce risk or increase returns is called _____.

    a. Dollar cost averaging
    b. Discounting
    c. Diversification
    d. Distribution

22. _____ risk refers to the impact that bad management decisions, other internal missteps, or external situations can have on a company's performance and on the value of investments in that company.

    a. Market
    b. Investment
    c. Financial
    d. Management

23. Under Regulation T, what is the maximum amount of the total purchase price of a stock for new purchases that a firm can lend a customer?

    a. 25%
    b. 50%
    c. 75%
    d. 100%

24. How often must firms notify employees of their business continuity or disaster recovery plans?

    a. Annually
    b. Semiannually
    c. Quarterly
    d. Monthly

25. Which of the following investments would be most suitable for an investor in a high tax bracket who wants to avoid paying any taxes on his investments?

    a. Corporate bond
    b. Municipal bond
    c. Mutual fund
    d. Preferred stock

26. What is margin in a brokerage account?

    a. The difference between the purchase price and the current value of each security.
    b. The difference between the beginning value and the current value of the entire account.
    c. Borrowed money that is used to purchase securities.
    d. Purchasing power in a cash account.

27. At what age does a UTMA account terminate?

    a. 18
    b. 19
    c. 20
    d. 21

28. _____ trading authority is when a person other than the account holder may invest without consulting the account holder about the price, amount, or type of security or the timing of the trades that are placed for the account.

    a. Discretionary
    b. Nondiscretionary
    c. Privileged
    d. Absolute

29. Which of the following would be a red flag when opening an account for a new client?

    a. No investment experience
    b. High annual income, but little or no savings
    c. Hesitant to give financial information
    d. Nervous or anxious when answering questions about objectives for the account

30. Dividing a larger transaction into smaller transactions to avoid triggering a reporting or recordkeeping requirement is called _____.

    a. Layering
    b. Fraud
    c. Structuring
    d. Laundering

31. Which of the following persons are considered corporate insiders?

    a. Officers
    b. Directors
    c. Employees
    d. All of the above

32. Systematic risk is also known as _____.

    a. Market risk
    b. Credit risk
    c. Liquidity risk
    d. Interest rate risk

33. What type of risk involves the chance that Congress will make unfavorable changes in tax laws?

    a. Market risk
    b. Event risk
    c. Tax risk
    d. Liquidity risk

34. Which of the following terms is a maneuver used by a company that increases the number of shares outstanding by exchanging a specified number of new shares of stock for each outstanding share?

    a. Stock dividend
    b. Stock split
    c. Stock valuation
    d. Stock buyback

35. Investing a fixed dollar amount in a security at fixed intervals is known as _____.

    a. Asset allocation
    b. Diversification
    c. Budgeting
    d. Dollar cost averaging

36. What is the name of the strategy where a company reduces the number of shares outstanding by exchanging a fractional amount of a new share for each outstanding share of stock?

    a. Stock dividend
    b. Stock split
    c. Reverse stock split
    d. Reverse stock dividend

37. If a company declares a 1:2 reverse stock split, how many shares will an investor with 200 shares own after the split?

    a. 100 shares
    b. 200 shares
    c. 300 shares
    d. 400 shares

38. _____ is an intangible asset that is the result of the acquisition of one company by another for a premium value.

    a. Target value
    b. Book value
    c. Acquisition value
    d. Goodwill

39. Which of the following characteristics are true of preferred stocks?

    I. Have a prior claim on the income and assets of the issuing firm
    II. Have fixed dividends
    III. Issued as an alternative to debt
    IV. Have an effect on EPS

    a. I and II
    b. I and III
    c. I, II, III
    d. I, II, III, IV

40. Dollar-denominated negotiable receipts for company stock of a foreign company held in trust in a foreign branch of a U.S. bank are _____.

- a. IPOs
- b. ADRs
- c. AMTs
- d. ATMs

41. Assuming rational market behavior, what should the opening price of ABC Corporation be on December 6?

> On Monday, December 5, after trading for that day ceased, ABC Corporation declared that it would pay an unanticipated $0.25 dividend, payable on December 15. The December 5 closing price of ABC Corporation stock is $25.34

- a. $25.34
- b. $25.09
- c. $25.59
- d. Not enough information given

42. An investor who owns 200 shares of XYZ Company, which is currently trading at $25.00, will be receiving a 20% stock dividend. What will the investor receive on the payment date?

- a. $1,000
- b. $100
- c. 20 shares of XYZ stock
- d. 40 shares of XYZ stock

43. How long must you hold an investment for it to be considered long term?

- a. 6 months
- b. 1 year
- c. 1 year and 1 day
- d. 2 years

44. What represents the amount of stockholders' capital in a firm?

- a. Assets
- b. Liabilities
- c. Equity
- d. Cash flow

45. Which financial statement provides a summary of the firm's cash flow and other events that caused changes in the cash position?

- a. Income statement
- b. Balance sheet
- c. Cash flow statement
- d. Annual report

46. What is the graph called that represents the relationship between a bond's term to maturity and its yield at a given point in time?

- a. Efficient frontier
- b. Point and figure chart
- c. Yield curve
- d. Bar chart

47. Which of the following mutual funds would be most likely to be passively managed?

a. Bond fund
b. Growth fund
c. Income fund
d. Index fund

48. An account in which customers with large portfolios pay a brokerage firm a flat annual fee that covers the cost of a money manager's services and the cost of commissions is called a _____ account.

a. Cash
b. Margin
c. Collateral
d. Wrap

Use the following information to answer the next two questions.

Net profit after taxes:	$18,000	Stockholder's Equity:	$170,000
Total revenues:	$615,000	Preferred dividends:	$5,000
Total assets:	$340,000	Number of common shares outstanding:	3,800
Current assets:	$280,000	Current liabilities:	$85,000
Earnings per share:	$4.75	Market price:	$49.50

49. What is the current ratio?

a. 2.92%
b. 3.29%
c. 5.29%
d. 10.59%

50. What is the book value per share?

a. $29.58
b. $43.42
c. $44.74
d. $46.10

51. Which of the following is the over-the-counter market?

a. NYSE
b. NASDAQ
c. CBOE
d. CBT

52. Which of the following is an example of a limit order?

a. An order to sell 100 shares of XYZ at the best price available
b. An order to sell 100 shares of XYZ (currently trading at $50) if the price drops to $45
c. An order to buy 100 shares of XYZ at the best price available
d. An order to buy 100 shares of XYZ at $40 or less

53. Which of the following is not required on an order ticket?

    a. Customer name
    b. Account number
    c. Order type
    d. Symbol

54. A stock trade executed on Friday, January 2, will settle on what date?

    a. Monday, January 5
    b. Tuesday, January 6
    c. Wednesday, January 7
    d. Thursday, January 8

55. In 2023, what is the maximum contribution that a 45-year-old may make into a traditional IRA?

    a. $2,000
    b. $3,500
    c. $6,500
    d. $7,500

56. What is the maximum annual contribution amount allowed in a Coverdell Education Savings Account (CESA)?

    a. $500
    b. $2,000
    c. $5,500
    d. $14,000

57. What is the tax consequence to an individual over the age of 59 ½ who withdraws a lump sum from his 401(K)?

    a. The amount withdrawn is considered income and is subject to income taxes at the individual's rate.
    b. The amount that is withdrawn is considered income and is subject to income taxes at the individual's current rate. Plus, he may be subject to a 10% penalty.
    c. He must pay a 10% penalty. Otherwise, there are no tax consequences.
    d. None of the above. A lump sum withdrawal from a 401(K) is not a taxable event.

58. How are capital gains and losses inside an IRA reported on an individual's income taxes each year?

    a. Neither gains nor losses within an IRA reported.
    b. Gains are not reported, but losses are reported on a Form 1099B to be used as a deduction.
    c. Both gains and losses are reported on Form 1099B.
    d. Gains and losses in an IRA are both reported on Form 1099B, but they are not subject to taxation.

59. An individual converts his $100,000 traditional IRA into a Roth IRA just before a major market decline causes the value to drop to $50,000. This investor should _____ the Roth IRA back to a traditional IRA to avoid paying taxes on the extra $50,000.

    a. De-convert
    b. Roll over
    c. Recharacterize
    d. Transfer

60. An option that is written against stock owned is a/an _____ option.

    a. Naked
    b. Covered
    c. Open
    d. Closed

61. How are gains and losses on options treated for tax purposes?

    a. They are treated as long-term gains or losses.
    b. They are treated as short-term gains or losses.
    c. They may be treated as either short-term or long-term gains or losses.
    d. Gains and losses on options are not taxable.

62. Which of the following statements are true regarding real estate investment trusts (REITs)?

    a. They are professionally managed.
    b. Allows smaller investors to participate in capital appreciation and income returns of real estate without owning any property.
    c. Returns can be very volatile.
    d. All of the above.

63. Which of the following corporate issues does an investor have the right to vote on as a common stockholder?

    a. Proposed stock splits
    b. Corporate bond issuance
    c. Election of the board of directors
    d. All of the above

64. All of the following are true of stockholder voting methods except that

    a. the statutory method involves an investor voting equal amounts of his or her votes for each of the candidates they would like to vote for.
    b. special circumstances may allow for a stockholder to vote more than one vote per share for each share he or she owns.
    c. the cumulative method involves an investor choosing to cast all of his or her votes for one candidate.
    d. there are two methods by which stockholders may cast their votes.

65. Which of the following describe the rights shareholders possesses?

    I. They retain an interest in residual assets that is proportionate to their investment in the event the corporation declares bankruptcy.

    II. They can access a corporation's financial information that would be otherwise held as confidential.

    III. They receive a shareholder list.

    IV. They can inspect a corporation's books and records.

a. II, III, and IV
b. I, III, and IV
c. I, II, and IV
d. III and IV

66. Which of the following is NOT true regarding the options of an investor who possesses a warrant to purchase common stock?

a. The investor must exercise the warrant before the stock's price rises above the subscription price.
b. The investor may sell the warrant to another investor.
c. The investor may exercise the warrant at any time prior to expiration to purchase common stock at the warrant's subscription price.
d. all of the above statements are true.

67. Which of the following duties does a transfer agent NOT perform?

a. Maintains the list of stockholders
b. Verifies owner identity in stock issuance
c. Verifies the validity and legality of a company's debt in a bond issuance
d. Handles new issuance of stock certificates

68. Which of the following economic indicators would be classified as a leading indicator?

    I. Stock market prices

    II. Corporate profit and loss

    III. Permits to build

    IV. Changes in borrowing (businesses and consumers)

a. I, II, III, and IV
b. I only
c. I, III, and IV
d. I and II

69. When considering a corporation's balance sheet, all of the following are categorized as *other assets* EXCEPT

a. trademarks.
b. patents.
c. property.
d. goodwill.

70. Of the following terms, which represents simply the value of a country's produced goods and services?

    a. Disintermediation
    b. Gross domestic product (GDP)
    c. Real gross domestic product (RGDP)
    d. Consumer price index (CPI)

71. Which of the following would be associated with the government's efforts to slow down the economy?

    I. Reduction in taxes
    II. Reduction spending
    III. Increase in taxes
    IV. Increase in spending

    a. I and II
    b. II and III
    c. III and IV
    d. I and IV

72. What is an order that enables the broker to have discretion regarding the timing of its execution and price called?

    a. Fill-or-kill order
    b. All-or-none order
    c. Market-on-open order
    d. Not-held order

73. An investor has sold short 275 shares of stock PPG at $26 per share. The market currently has PPG trading at $11 per share. The investor sees news of the company that may indicate a price increase over the short term. Which of the following would provide this investor with guaranteed protection against missing a purchase of PPG at a level at which he or she can still make a profit given the short position?

    a. Buy 275 PPG at $21 stop
    b. Unknown without more information
    c. Buy 275 PPG at $32 stop
    d. None of the above

74. When orders have the same price, what is the order of prioritization for executing each?

    I. Parity
    II. Precedence
    III. Priority

    a. I and II
    b. II, I, and III
    c. III, II, and I
    d. I, II, and III

75. Which of the following are considered to be actions falling under the role of a dealer?

      I. Charges a commission for their services
      II. Participates in the trade by trading in and out of his or her own account
      III. Fills the role of market maker
      IV. May facilitate only the order execution for a customer

  a. II only
  b. I, II, and III
  c. I and IV
  d. II and III

Answer Key and Explanations for Test #2

1. D: A member shall promptly report the complaint, no later than 30 calendar days after the member knows or should have known of the existence of the written complaint.

2. C: Correspondence means any written communication (including electronic) that is distributed to 25 or fewer retail investors within any 30-day period.

3. C: Any gift from or to a member or person associated with a member may not exceed $100 per year.

4. D: Front running is the prohibited activity of a registered representative trading based on non-public information in his or her own account prior to the information becoming public to other traders. Market timing is the practice of timing or calculating the market's low and high points, buying when it is low and selling when it is high. Rebalancing refers to adjusting a customer's portfolio to return to previously set ratios of investment types. Churning involves a broker, or someone trading on behalf of a customer, processing excessive transactions with the goal of increasing their commissions from trades.

5. D: Member firms must disclose, in writing, to all new customers that they may obtain more information about SIPC, including the brochure, by contacting SIPC and must also provide the website address and telephone number of SIPC.

6. C: The term research report refers to printed or processed analysis covering individual companies or industries.

7. B: If only a nominal sum is paid, the body copy of the material does not need to clearly state that it is a paid testimonial. If more than a nominal sum is paid, however, the fact that it is a paid testimonial must be indicated.

8. B: Investment firms and advisers are required to register with the SEC, FINRA, and the office of the securities regulator of the state in which they are doing business. Firms and advisors can register for all three using SEC Form BD.

9. D: Prior to the Options Disclosure Document (ODD) being delivered, a registered representative must limit discussion to general descriptions of the options. Solicitations and trades are not allowed prior to delivery of the ODD.

10. A: A municipal security advertisement that concerns the facilities, services, or skills with respect to municipal securities of such broker, dealer, or municipal securities dealer or of another broker, dealer, or municipal securities dealer is the definition of a professional advertisement.

11. C: A member may not publish a research report regarding a subject company for which the member acted as manager or co-manager of an IPO for40 calendar days following the date of the offering.

12. C: A registered principal (or supervisory analyst) must approve all third-party research reports distributed by a member. A registered principal (or supervisory analyst) does not need to approve independent third-party research reports.

13. B: A mutual fund account is covered by SIPC rather than FDIC. Bank savings, checking, and money market accounts as well as certificates of deposits are covered by FDIC.

14. B: The FDIC covers up to $250,000 per depositor per insured bank for each account ownership category. The SIPC protects customers of brokerage firms up to a total of $500,000 across all accounts but not per account.

15. D: In TY 2023, $17,000 is the maximum amount that may be gifted within one calendar year to avoid taxation.

16. A: An initial public offering refers to the event of a company first offering its shares for sale to the public. Market offerings and initial sales offerings are not generally accepted terms for this event. A rights offering refers to a group of rights, a kind of option, offered to shareholders to purchase more shares.

17. B: Congress created the Securities and Exchange Commission (SEC) under the Securities Exchange Act of 1934. The Securities Act of 1933 regulates the stock market. The Investment Company Act of 1940 regulates the organization of investment companies. The Investment Advisers Act of 1940 defines an investment advisor.

18. C: Liabilities are not required financial information on a new account application. Net worth, annual income, and investment goals are required pieces of financial information to open a brokerage account with any firm.

19. B: The length of time an investor *plans* or *expects* to keep an investment is known as the time horizon. The holding period refers to the length of time that an asset is *actually* held. During an IPO process, the SEC restricts the marketing department of the company from publicizing any information about the IPO to avoid insider trading. Calendar period does not refer to any specific investment concept.

20. D: A zero coupon bond would not be appropriate for an investor with a capital growth objective. Bonds and annuities are better suited for investors with a conservative or fixed income objective. Unit investment trusts are similar to mutual funds in that they offer a variety of portfolios to invest in, including growth. Common stocks are perfect for growth investors as they provide the opportunity to invest directly in the company to maximize capital gains. Growth mutual funds offer investors a single price for a growth-focused portfolio consisting of any number of companies.

21. C: Investing in multiple investment vehicles within a portfolio to reduce risk or increase returns is called diversification. An investor engages in dollar-cost averaging by purchasing a fixed-dollar amount of a given security at set intervals, such as monthly, to smooth out the volatility. Discounting involves calculating the net present value of a distribution of funds that is to take place in the future. A distribution is the payout (interest, dividend, etc.) from an investment.

22. D: Management risk refers to the impact that bad management decisions or other internal missteps can have on a company's performance and on the value of investments in that company. Market risk, or systematic risk, is the potential for loss due to the performance of the financial market. Investment risk is the risk that an investment's performance will be worse than expected. Financial risk is a generic term describing a variety of risk types, including credit risk, liquidity risk, and operational risk.

23. B: Under Regulation T, the maximum amount of the total purchase price of a stock for new purchases that a firm can lend a customer is 50%.

123

24. A: Firms must notify employees of their business continuity or disaster recovery plans at least annually.

25. B: A municipal bond would be the most suitable investment for an investor in a high tax bracket who wants to avoid paying any taxes on his investments. Municipal bonds are tax-exempt, so investors do not have to pay taxes on the interest from the bonds. By contrast, investors do have to pay taxes on the interest from corporate bonds, mutual funds, and preferred stocks.

26. C: Margin in a brokerage account is borrowed money that is used to purchase securities. The difference between the purchase price and the current value is called capital gains. The difference between the beginning value and the current value of an account would also be considered capital gains. Purchasing power is all available funds (unsettled, liquid, and borrowed) that can be used to purchase securities.

27. D: A UTMA account terminates when the minor reaches the age of 21.

28. A: Discretionary trading authority is when a person other than the account holder may invest without consulting the account holder about the price, amount, or type of security or the timing of the trades that are placed for the account.

29. D: A person who acts nervously or anxiously when answering questions about their objectives would raise a red flag when opening an account for a new client. It is common to find new investors who have no experience in the financial markets. While having a client with poor spending habits is unfortunate, it is not a sign of acting in bad faith. Customers can sometimes be skeptical about providing personal details, especially financial information.

30. C: Dividing a larger transaction into smaller transactions to avoid triggering a reporting or recordkeeping requirement is called structuring or smurfing. Layering is the second step in money laundering in which the criminal conceals the source of their money by executing multiple transactions. Fraud is an umbrella term for criminal activity such as tax fraud, credit card fraud, or securities fraud. Money laundering is the process of taking money that was generated from illegal activity and making it appear that it was earned legitimately.

31. D: Officers, directors, and employees are all persons that are considered to be corporate insiders.

32. A: Systematic risk, also known as market risk, affects the entire market rather than a specific security or industry. Credit risk is the risk that a lender takes on, arising from the uncertainty of whether a borrower will be able to repay what they have been loaned. Liquidity risk is the risk that an investor, firm, or institution may suffer a capital loss from having to liquidate assets at an unfavorable time (e.g., selling off assets at lower prices because funds are needed immediately). Interest rate risk is the risk of investments losing value due to changes in prevailing interest rates.

33. C: Tax risk is the risk that the state or federal governments will make unfavorable changes to tax law. Market risk is the potential for loss due to the performance of the financial market. Event risk is the risk of an unexpected event negatively affecting an investment's value. Liquidity risk is the risk that an investor, firm, or institution may suffer a capital loss from having to liquidate assets at an unfavorable time (e.g., selling off assets at lower prices because funds are needed immediately).

34. B: A stock split is a maneuver used by a company that increases the number of shares outstanding by exchanging a specified number of new shares of stock for each outstanding share. A

124

stock dividend is a distribution made by a company to its shareholders of additional shares of stock. Stock valuation is the process of determining the value of the shares of a company's stock. When a company uses its capital to repurchase shares it has previously issued, this is called a stock buyback.

35. D: Dollar-cost averaging is the process of investing a fixed dollar amount in a security at fixed intervals.

36. C: A reverse stock split is the strategy where a company reduces the number of shares outstanding by exchanging a fractional amount of a new share for each outstanding share of stock. A stock split is a maneuver used by a company to increase the number of shares outstanding by exchanging a specified number of new shares of stock for each outstanding share. A stock dividend is a distribution made by a company to its shareholders of additional shares of stock. There is no such thing as a reverse stock dividend.

37. A: If a company declares a 1:2 reverse stock split, an investor with 200 shares will own 100 shares after the split.

38. D: Goodwill is an intangible asset that is the result of the acquisition of one company by another for a premium value. Market value is what others are willing to pay for an asset on the open market. The book value is the difference between a company's total assets and total liabilities. Acquisition value or acquisition cost is the price paid for the acquisition of an asset, including all taxes, fees, charges, and other expenses.

39. C: Preferred stocks have a prior claim on the income and assets of the issuing firm, have fixed dividends, and are issued as an alternative to debt, but do not have an effect on EPS.

40. B: American depositary receipts (ADRs) are dollar-denominated negotiable receipts for company stock of a foreign company held in trust in a foreign branch of a U.S. bank. An initial public offering (IPO) refers to the event of a company first offering its shares for sale to the public. An alternative minimum tax (AMT) is a backup tax designed to ensure that high earners cannot use tax avoidance strategies to lower their tax liability below a certain level. Automated teller machines (ATMs) are machines that can be used to deposit or withdraw funds from a customer's bank account.

41. C: The opening price of ABC Corporation should be $25.59 on December 6 ($25.34 + $0.25). Since a dividend of $0.25 per share was announced after the market closed on December 5, each share became more valuable by that amount. It's always possible for stocks to not trade at what they're supposed to, given a free market, but assuming rational market behavior, ABC stock would trade at the sum of its closing price ($25.34) plus the declared dividend amount ($0.25): $25.59.

42. D: The investor will receive 40 shares of XYZ stock on the payment date. A stock dividend is a distribution made by a company to its shareholders of additional shares of stock. Since the company is issuing each shareholder an extra $\frac{1}{5}$ share (20%) for every share owned, an individual who holds 200 shares will receive $200 \times \frac{1}{5} = 40$ new shares of XYZ Company.

43. C: An investment must be held for one year and one day to be considered long term. Anything less is considered short term.

44. C: Equity represents the amount of stockholders' capital in a firm. Assets are resources held by the company that have immediate value or that will provide a future benefit. A liability is an obligation, financial or otherwise, that the company owes to a person or business entity. Cash flow is the amount of cash moving into and out of a company.

45. C: The cash flow statement provides a summary of a company's cash flow and other events that caused changes in their cash position. The income statement reports a company's revenue over a specified time period, along with the expenses the company incurred to generate that revenue. The balance sheet is a summary report of a company's assets and liabilities, along with stockholder equity. An annual report is a document describing operations and financial position that every company listed on the stock market must provide to its shareholders.

46. C: The yield curve is the graph that represents the relationship between a bond's term to maturity and its yield at a given point in time. The efficient frontier is the upper limit of how much growth a portfolio can expect to see given its level of acceptable risk. A point-and-figure chart plots price movement without looking at time. Bar charts show multiple prices over time.

47. D: An index mutual fund is the most likely to be passively managed because it seeks to mimic the performance of a specified index by holding the same stocks as the chosen index. Bond, growth, and income funds are all actively managed by portfolio managers who pick and choose different securities depending on the type of fund and the investment goal.

48. D: A wrap account is an account in which customers with large portfolios pay a brokerage firm a flat annual fee that covers the cost of a money manager's services and the cost of commissions.

49. B: The current ratio is 3.29%.

$$\frac{\$280,000 \text{ (current assets)}}{\$85,000 \text{ (current liabilities)}} = 3.29\%$$

50. B: The book value per share is $43.42.

$$\frac{\$170,000 \text{ (stockholder equity)} - \$5,000 \text{ (preferred dividends)}}{3,800 \text{ (outstanding shares of common stock)}} = \$43.42$$

51. B: NASDAQ is the over-the-counter (OTC) market.

52. D: An order to sell a stock at a specific price or better is a limit order. Answers A and C are examples of a market order. Answer B is an example of a stop order.

53. A: The customer's name is not required on an order ticket. The type of order, account number, and symbol are all required items on an order ticket.

54. B: Stock trades ordinarily settle on a T+2 schedule, meaning that the settlement date is two business days following the trade date (T). Therefore, a stock trade executed on Friday, January 2, would settle on Tuesday, January 6, since weekends do not count as business days.

55. C: In TY 2023, the maximum contribution that a 45-year-old may make into a traditional IRA is $6,500.

56. B: The maximum annual contribution amount allowed in a Coverdell Education Savings Account (CESA) in TY 2023 is $2,000.

57. A: The tax consequence to an individual over the age of 59 ½ who withdraws a lump sum from his 401(k) is that the amount withdrawn is considered income and is subject to income taxes at the individual's current rate.

58. A: Capital gains and losses inside an IRA are not reported on an individual's income taxes each year.

59. C: An individual converts his $100,000 traditional IRA into a Roth IRA just before a major market decline causes the value to drop to $50,000. This investor should recharacterize the Roth IRA back to a traditional IRA to avoid paying taxes on the extra $50,000.

60. B: An option that is written against stock owned is a covered option. When a trader sells an options contract without actually owning the underlying asset, this is called a naked option. An options order is classified as buy-to-open when a trader is seeking to establish a new position (call or put) in a given option. In contrast, an options order is classified as buy-to-close when the trader is seeking to close out an existing position.

61. B: All gains and losses on options are treated as short-term gains or losses for tax purposes.

62. D: All of the statements are true. REITS are professionally managed, allow smaller investors to participate in capital appreciation and income returns of real estate without owning any property, and returns can be very volatile.

63. D: Common stockholders have the right by ownership to vote on proposed stock splits, corporate bond issuance, and the election of the corporation's board of directors.

64. B: Stockholders are allowed only one vote for every share owned. The statutory method provides for voting equal amounts of votes over more than one candidate, the cumulative method involves casting all votes for one candidate, and there are two methods for stockholder voting, statutory and cumulative.

65. B: Shareholders will retain proportionate interest in residual assets in the event of bankruptcy, may receive a list of shareholders, and may inspect a corporation's books and records. They do not have the right to access and review a corporation's confidential financial information.

66. A: A warrant is valid for a set period of time, and does not become invalid because of movement in the market price of the stock. An investor who holds a warrant may sell the warrant to another investor or exercise the warrant to purchase common stock at the subscription price.

67. C: A transfer agent does not verify company debt; this is the role of the registrar. A transfer agent does maintain the list of stockholders, verifies the correct issuance of shares, and handles the new issuance of stock certificates.

68. C: Stock market prices, permits for building, and changes in business and consumer borrowing are all considered to be leading economic indicators in that they each act as signals of an impending change to the economy and, accordingly, can be observed prior to the actual change. Corporate profits and losses are considered to be lagging economic indicators in that these types of effects are more observable after the change in the economy has already occurred.

69. C: Property, when categorized on a corporation's balance sheet, is considered a fixed asset. Other assets can include a corporation's trademarks, patents, and goodwill.

70. B: The value of a country's produced goods and services is its gross domestic product (GDP). Disintermediation involves investors moving their money from low-yielding investments to higher-yielding ones. The real GDP is a deflation- and inflation-adjusted version of the value of a country's produced goods and services. The consumer price index (CPI) is a tool utilized to measure the rise and fall of overall prices in the country by monitoring the price changes of a specific group of goods and services chosen for their high degree of use in individual lives.

71. B: The government, in moving to slow down the economy, would reduce spending and increase taxes so as to reduce overall demand for goods and services and decrease the level of money that consumers have access to.

72. D: A not-held order gives discretion to the broker as to timing and price for the order's execution. A fill-or-kill order must be executed immediately upon receipt, or it must be cancelled. An all-or-none order indicates that the investor would like all of the securities bought or sold in the transaction or none at all. A market-on-open order indicates the investor's wish to have it executed right at the opening of the market or as close to it as possible.

73. A: A buy 275 PPG at $21 stop order will allow this investor to pay no more than $21 per share in filling the short position, which has a sell price of $26 per share. A profit will still be made. Conversely, a buy 275 PPG at $32 stop order will enable their order to go as high as $32 a share before being executed, thus potentially eliminating a profit being made by this investor on the short position.

74. C: When orders come in at the same price, they are filled based on priority (first in, first executed), precedence (the larger of the orders is executed first), and parity (if all orders are the same, outstanding orders and shares are divided and shared).

75. D: Actions falling under the role of a dealer include participating in trades by trading in and out of his or her own account, such as using securities in the account to fill a buy order or buying securities for the account to fill a customer's sell order. Further, making a market in a security is also an action performed by a dealer. Conversely, a broker simply facilitates order execution for a customer, while not participating in the transaction, and charges a commission for their services.

SIE Practice Test #3

1. Which of the following are considered institutional investors?

    a. A governmental entity

    b. An employee benefit plan that meets the requirement of Section 403(b) or Section 457 of the Internal Revenue Code and has at least 100 participants

    c. A qualified plan as defined in Section 3(a)(12)(C) of the Exchange Act and that has at least 100 participants

    d. All of the above

2. What is the time-of-day restriction when placing cold calls (telemarketing)?

    a. Before 8:00 a.m. and after 9:00 p.m. (local time of the caller's location)

    b. Before 8:00 a.m. and after 9:00 p.m. (local time of the called party's location)

    c. Before 8:00 a.m. and after 8:00 p.m. (local time of the caller's location)

    d. Before 8:00 a.m. and after 8:00 p.m. (local time of the called party's location)

3. Which of the following would be considered a breakpoint sale?

    a. A customer purchasing $150,000 in multiple mutual funds and paying the full sales charge of each.

    b. A customer receiving a 20% discount on an equity trade.

    c. A customer purchasing a municipal bond above par.

    d. A customer purchasing a corporate bond below par.

4. Which of the following are prohibited activities?

    a. Churning

    b. Front running

    c. Insider trading

    d. All of the above

5. Which of the following is not a general consideration regarding communications with the public about variable life insurance and variable annuities?

    a. Prospectus delivery

    b. Product Identification

    c. Liquidity

    d. Claims about guarantees

6. Which of the following is true regarding recommendations?

    a. Must have a reasonable basis

    b. The market price at the time of the recommendation must be shown

    c. Supporting information should be provided or offered

    d. All of the above

7. When must a Form U5 be filed?

    a. At the time of employment with a member firm

    b. At the time of termination of employment from a member firm

    c. Annually for each registered representative employed by a member firm

    d. Every three years for each registered representative employed by a member firm

8. When must political contributions be disclosed to the MSRB?

a. Quarterly
b. Semiannually
c. Annually
d. Never

9. Which of the following is false regarding options-related advertisements?

a. Must be approved in advance by a Registered Options Principal
b. Copies must be retained by the member firm
c. Records containing the name of the persons who created and approved the advertisement must be kept
d. FINRA never needs to approve options-related advertisements

10. Before a registered representative may recommend the purchase or exchange of a deferred variable annuity, he or she must have a reasonable basis to believe all of the following except:

a. The transaction is suitable
b. The customer will not need the funds invested
c. The customer would benefit from certain features such as tax-deferred growth
d. The customer has been informed of various features such as a surrender period and surrender charge

11. A member may not publish a research report regarding a subject company for which the member acted as manager or co-manager of a secondary offering for _____ days following the date of the offering.

a. 10 calendar days
b. 10 business days
c. 20 calendar days
d. 20 business days

12. Which of the following must be disclosed in a research report?

a. Ownership and material conflicts of interest
b. Receipt of compensation
c. If the member was making a market in the subject company's securities at the time that research report was published
d. All of the above

13. What is the tentative prospectus circulated by the underwriters of a new of stock that is pending approval the SEC?

a. Red herring
b. IPO
c. Registration statement
d. Private placement

14. Beginning in TY 2023, what is the basic exclusion limit on tax-free transfers during life or at death (the unification of gift and estate taxes)?

  a. $11,140,000
  b. $11,580,000
  c. $12,060,000
  d. $12,920,000

15. What is the cost basis of securities given as a gift?

  a. The average of the high and low prices on the date of the gift
  b. The purchase price of the securities when they were originally bought
  c. The average of the current market price and the price originally paid
  d. None of the above

16. Which of the following is not a purpose of the Securities Act of 1933?

  a. Require that investors receive financial and other significant information
  b. Guarantee the financial information received by investors is accurate
  c. Prohibit deceit, misrepresentations, and fraud in the sale of securities
  d. Require the registration of securities

17. Which of the following is an SRO?

  a. New York Stock Exchange
  b. NASDAQ Stock Market
  c. Chicago Board of Options
  d. All of the above

18. Which of the following items should not be taken into consideration when determining investment suitability?

  a. Annual income
  b. Investment experience
  c. Net worth
  d. None of the above

19. Which of the following investments would be most appropriate for an investor with an objective of capital preservation?

  a. Preferred stock
  b. Certificate of deposit
  c. Municipal bond
  d. Corporate bond

20. What is another name for the investment objective of total return?

  a. Growth
  b. Income
  c. Growth and income
  d. Preservation of capital

21. Which of the following scenarios is the best example of diversification?

   a. An investor buys 1,000 shares of ABC stock at $25 per share
   b. An investor who invests $25,000 in one corporate bond
   c. An investor who invests $25,000 in a large cap growth mutual fund
   d. An investor who invests a total of $25,000 between stocks, bonds, and mutual funds.

22. Which of the following statements is false regarding modern portfolio theory?

   a. It is a scientific approach to measuring risk.
   b. It guarantees against long-term losses.
   c. It involves calculating projected returns of various portfolio combinations.
   d. It is the concept of minimizing risk by combining volatile and price-stable investment in a single portfolio.

23. Which of the following are examples of information security to protect customers' personal information?

   a. Encrypted email
   b. Password-protected laptops
   c. Printing only the last four digits of Social Security numbers on documents
   d. All of the above

24. Which of the following investments would be the least suitable for an elderly investor who is risk averse?

   a. Municipal bond
   b. Corporate bond
   c. Mutual fund
   d. Common stock

25. Which of the following investors would be best suited to invest in US Treasuries?

   a. A 25-year-old interested in speculative investments
   b. A 25-year-old with an investment objective of growth
   c. A retired individual with an investment objective of growth
   d. A retired individual with an investment objective of income

26. In a joint tenancy with rights of survivorship (JTWROS) account, what happens to the assets when the first person dies?

   a. 50% of the assets are transferred to an estate account for the deceased person
   b. 100% of the assets remain with the surviving co-account holder
   c. 50% of the assets are transferred directly to the deceased person's heirs
   d. 100% of the assets are transferred to an estate account for the deceased person

27. Who is/are the authorized person(s) on an estate account?

   a. An attorney
   b. A financial advisor
   c. The heir(s)
   d. The personal representative(s)

28. How long must a member firm maintain client account statements?

a. 1 year
b. 3 years
c. 6 years
d. 10 years

29. Which of the following account activities in a newly opened account would raise suspicions as a possible money laundering activity?

a. Multiple deposits that are immediately wired out of the account to a foreign bank.
b. Multiple deposits from other financial institutions that fund the purchases of several securities that remain in the account.
c. One large deposit that is only partially invested in securities.
d. Funds received via Fedwire

30. _____ is the process that criminals use to try to hide or disguise the source of their illegal money by converting it into funds that appear legitimate.

a. Layering
b. Structuring
c. Laundering
d. Blackmail

31. The practice of buying and selling stocks rapidly throughout the day in the hope that the stocks will continue climbing or falling in value for the seconds to minutes that they are owned allowing for quick profits to be made is called _____.

a. Buy and hold
b. Active trading
c. Market timing
d. Day trading

32. Which of the following investments would not be a suitable recommendation for an IRA?

a. Common stock
b. Corporate bond
c. Municipal bond
d. Mutual fund

33. The possibility of higher prices in the future reducing the amount of goods or services that may be bought is known as _____.

a. Market risk
b. Purchasing power risk
c. Financial risk
d. Interest rate risk

34. What is the name for stocks that have been sold and then repurchased (and held) by the issuing firm?

a. Outstanding stock
b. Treasury stock
c. Issued stock
d. Restricted stock

35. A _____ is an equity investment representing ownership in a corporation.
   a. Corporate bond
   b. Common stock
   c. Warrant
   d. Right

36. A company declares a 2:1 stock split. An investor who currently owns 100 shares of stock will have how many shares after the split?
   a. 50 shares
   b. 100 shares
   c. 150 shares
   d. 200 shares

37. Selling a security to generate a loss and then immediately buying the security back is a _____.
   a. Capital loss
   b. Whipsaw
   c. Wash sale
   d. Tax loss sale

38. Which of the following is an option issued by a given company to buy one or more shares of common stock in that company at a price initially above the market price?
   a. Right
   b. Warrant
   c. Call
   d. Put

39. The market in which securities are traded after they have been issued is the _____?
   a. Primary market
   b. Money market
   c. Super market
   d. Secondary market

40. Which of the following risks are associated with investing internationally?
   a. Foreign currency risk
   b. Market risk
   c. Event risk
   d. All of the above

41. What is the last date that ABC Corporation stock can be purchased to receive the dividend?

   On November 1, ABC Corporation declared a $0.25 dividend to shareholders of record on Monday, December 5, payable on December 15.

   a. December 1
   b. December 5
   c. December 12
   d. December 15

42. A customer purchases 100 shares of ABC stock at $35/share and pays $85 in commissions. What is the cost basis?

a. $3,415
b. $3,500
c. $3,585
d. $3,600

43. _____ represents the resources of a company.

a. Assets
b. Liabilities
c. Equity
d. Cash flow

44. Which financial statement shows the company's assets, liabilities, and shareholders' equity?

a. Income statement
b. Balance sheet
c. Cash flow statement
d. Annual report

45. Municipal bonds backed by the full faith and credit, and taxing power, of the issuer are called _____.

a. Revenue bonds
b. General obligation bonds
c. Agency bonds
d. Treasury notes

46. Which of the following statements is false regarding an upward-sloping yield curve?

a. It indicates that yields tend to increase with longer maturities.
b. The longer the time span until maturity, the greater potential for price volatility.
c. The longer the time span until maturity, the greater the risk for loss.
d. It indicates that short-term rates are higher than long-term rates.

47. What is the measure of bond price volatility that captures both price and reinvestment risks indicating how a bond will react to different interest rate environments?

a. Yield
b. Duration
c. Immunization
d. Beta

Use the following information to answer the next two questions.

Net profit after taxes:	$18,000	Stockholder's Equity:	$170,000
Total revenues:	$615,000	Preferred dividends:	$5,000
Total assets:	$340,000	Number of common shares outstanding:	3,800
Current assets:	$280,000	Current liabilities:	$85,000
Earnings per share:	$4.75	Market price:	$49.50

48. What is the return on assets (ROA)?

    a. 2.92%
    b. 3.29%
    c. 4.76%
    d. 5.29%

49. What is the return on equity (ROE)?

    a. 2.92%
    b. 5.29%
    c. 10.42%
    d. 10.59%

50. What is the term for the standard of conduct or moral judgment?

    a. Values
    b. Ethics
    c. Conscience
    d. Golden rule

51. An order to buy or sell a stock at the best available price when the order is placed is a _____ order.

    a. Limit
    b. Stop
    c. Market
    d. Stop limit

52. Which of the following is an example of a stop order?

    a. An order to sell 100 shares of XYZ at the best price available
    b. An order to sell 100 shares of XYZ (currently trading at $50) if the price drops to $45
    c. An order to buy 100 shares of XYZ at the best price available
    d. An order to buy 100 shares of XYZ at $40 or less

53. It is the responsibility of the _____ to ensure that a customer receives the correct breakpoint.

    a. Registered representative
    b. Customer
    c. Mutual fund company
    d. Broker-dealer

54. A stock trade executed on Wednesday, December 31, will settle on what date?

    a. Monday, January 5
    b. Tuesday, January 6
    c. Wednesday, January 7
    d. Thursday, January 8

55. What is the maximum amount that may be contributed to a 529 plan in TY 2023?

    a. $2,000
    b. $5,500
    c. $6,500
    d. $17,000

56. What is the tax consequence to an individual who rolls over his 401(K) directly to a traditional IRA?

    a. The amount that is rolled over is considered income and is subject to income taxes at the individual's rate.

    b. The amount that is rolled over is considered income and is subject to income taxes at the individual's current rate. Plus, if the individual is under age 59 ½, he may be subject to a 10% penalty.

    c. If the individual is under age 59 ½, he must pay a 10% penalty. Otherwise, there are no tax consequences.

    d. None of the above. A direct rollover from a 401(K) to a traditional IRA is not a taxable event.

57. An individual who withdraws a lump sum from a qualified plan can avoid income taxes and penalties if the entire amount is rolled over into a traditional IRA within _____ days.

    a. 30 days
    b. 45 days
    c. 60 days
    d. 90 days

58. By what date must an individual take his first required minimum distribution (RMD)?

    a. At any time in the year he turns 70.5
    b. By April 15 in the year following the year he turns 70.5
    c. By December 31 in the year he turns 70.5
    d. On the date that he turns 70.5

59. What is the income limit for single individuals to contribute to a Roth IRA in TY 2023?

    a. $139,000
    b. $144,000
    c. $153,000
    d. $161,000

60. The price at which you can buy a security with a call is the _____.

    a. Purchase price
    b. Sale price
    c. Offering price
    d. Strike price

61. Which of the following statements is true regarding the maximum profit and loss that the writer of an uncovered call option may realize?

    a. The maximum profit is the premium amount.
    b. The maximum loss is the premium amount.
    c. The maximum profit is limitless.
    d. The maximum loss is the strike price times the number of shares.

62. Which of the following can be defined as a *security*?

    a. Fixed annuities
    b. Variable annuities
    c. Individual retirement accounts (IRAs)
    d. All of the above

63. Which of the following are true of the term *equity*?

    I. It is interchangeable with the term *stock*.

    II. It provides the investor with ownership stake in the issuing corporation.

    III. The shares do not mature and are therefore perpetual.

    IV. A corporation's goal in selling shares is to create capital.

  a. II, III, and IV

  b. II only

  c. I, II, III, and IV

  d. I and II

64. What is stock that has been authorized for sale and sold to investors (regardless of its current ownership) considered to be?

  a. Issued stock

  b. Authorized stock

  c. Treasury stock

  d. Outstanding stock

65. Which of the following actions regarding stock PIX would be considered a violation for any registered representative?

  a. Rushing a customer to purchase stock PIX specifically to qualify prior to the ex-dividend date

  b. Making a customer recommendation to purchase stock PIX simply to benefit from a pending dividend payment

  c. Recommending a purchase of stock PIX to a customer by highlighting the pending dividend payment as an incentive while neglecting to educate him or her on the stock's fundamentals, appropriateness, risks, and rewards

  d. All of the above are violations.

66. Corporation PIX is behind on paying out a dividend on its 6% cumulative preferred stock. It has not paid a dividend for the past two years as well as the current year. What is the amount per share the owners of these shares should be paid to be current, and which of the following should be paid their dividend first: owners of cumulative preferred shares or common shareholders?

  a. $12 per share, cumulative preferred shareholders

  b. $18 per share, common stock shareholders

  c. $180 per share, cumulative preferred shareholders

  d. $18 per share, cumulative preferred shareholders

67. What would the calculated current yield be for an investor given the following information?

    Investor buys 200 shares of stock PIX @ $45 per share.

    Stock PIX is currently trading @ $52 per share.

    Co. PIX pays a quarterly dividend of $1.25.

  a. 9.6%

  b. 2.8%

  c. 2.4%

  d. 11%

68. The Federal Reserve acts to guide and control the monetary policy of the country. Which of the following are actions it might take to do that?

   a. Alter the level of money that is circulated.
   b. Actively participate in open market transactions involving US government securities.
   c. Publicly communicate its views regarding the economy.
   d. All of the above actions will work.

69. Which of the following is a consequence of the Federal Reserve increasing the discount rate?

   a. A slowing of the economy
   b. Demand increases
   c. Reduction in all other rates
   d. None of the above

70. Of the different types of economic indicators, which type acts to provide confirmation of the state of the economy based on indicators that occur for a period of time after a change in its direction occurs?

   a. Lagging indicators
   b. Coincident indicators
   c. Leading indicators
   d. All of the above

71. What is the type of company whose earnings are easily affected and impacted by whatever the state of the overall economy is?

   a. Defensive
   b. Growth
   c. Cyclical
   d. None of the above

72. All of the following are true of market orders except that

   a. they will be executed at the best possible price available.
   b. they guarantee a maximum or minimum executed price for the order.
   c. they can either be a buy or sell order.
   d. they guarantee that the order will be executed immediately upon being introduced to the market.

73. An investor places an order to buy 250 PPG 62.15 GTC DNR. The stock closes the prior day at 63.10. Further, the stock goes ex dividend for 0.15 and accordingly will open with the market the next day at 62.95. Given these developments, which of the following depicts what the investor's buy order will be as of market opening the next day?

   a. Buy 250 PPG 62.95 GTC DNR
   b. Buy 250 PPG 62.15 GTC DNR
   c. Buy 250 PPG 62 GTC
   d. None of the above

74. What is a dealer violation involving a dealer not honoring his or her published NASDAQ quote called?

   a. Backing away
   b. Pulling out
   c. Canceling
   d. Revocation

75. What is an investment that involves investors receiving interest and principal payments on a monthly basis as a result of individual mortgages being paid down known as?

   a. A pass-through
   b. Separate Trading of Registered Interest and Principal of Securities (STRIP)
   c. Collateralized mortgage obligation
   d. TIPS

Answer Key and Explanations for Test #3

1. D: A governmental entity, an employee benefit plan that meets the requirement of Section 403(b) or Section 457 of the Internal Revenue Code and has at least 100 participants, and a qualified plan, as defined in Section 3(a)(12)(C) of the Exchange Act, that has at least 100 participants are all considered institutional investors.

2. B: The time-of-day restriction when placing cold calls is before 8:00 a.m. and after 9:00 p.m. (local time of the called party's location).

3. A: A breakpoint sale takes place when an investor invests in investment company shares at a level below where the sales charge would be reduced (the breakpoint). Equities, municipal bonds, and corporate bonds are not investment company shares.

4. D: Churning, front-running, and insider trading are all prohibited activities. Churning involves a broker, or someone trading on behalf of a customer, processing excessive transactions with the goal of increasing their commissions from trades. Front-running is an unethical, and generally illegal, activity in which a broker makes advantageous trades by using non-public information about an impending transaction. Insider trading is the illegal use of non-public information about a company by a person within that company to profit in the stock market.

5. A: Prospectus delivery is not a general consideration regarding communications with the public about variable life insurance and variable annuities. Product identification, liquidity, and claims about guarantees are general considerations.

6. D: When making recommendations, there must be a reasonable basis, the market price at the time of the recommendation must be shown, and supporting information should be provided or offered.

7. B: A Form U5 must be filed when a registered individual's employment with a member firm is terminated.

8. A: Political contributions must be reported to the MSRB by the last day of the month following the end of each calendar quarter (January 31, April 30, July 31, and October 31).

9. D: FINRA's Advertising Regulation Department *must* approve certain options communications with the public. Options-related advertisements also must be approved in advance by a Registered Options Principal, have copies retained by the member firm, and keep records containing the name of the persons who created and approved the advertisement (see FINRA Rule 2220).

10. B: A registered representative (RR) does not need to have a reasonable basis to believe that the customer will not need the funds invested before recommending the purchase or exchange of a deferred variable annuity. The RR must have a reasonable basis to believe that the transaction is suitable, that the customer would benefit from certain features such as tax-deferred growth, and that the customer has been informed of various features such as a surrender period and surrender charge.

11. A: A member may not publish a research report regarding a subject company for which the member acted as manager or co-manager of a secondary offering for 10 calendar days following the date of the offering.

12. D: Ownership and material conflicts of interest, receipt of compensation, and if the member was making a market in the subject company's securities at the time that research report was published must all be disclosed in a research report.

13. A: The tentative, or preliminary, prospectus circulated by the underwriters of a new issue of stock that is pending approval by the SEC is known as a red herring. An initial public offering (IPO) refers to the event of a company first offering its shares for sale to the public. Before shares can be offered to the public, a company must file a registration statement, or prospectus, with the SEC. A private placement is a securities transaction in which shares are sold only to a select set of entities.

14. D: Beginning in TY 2023, the basic exclusion limit on tax-free transfers during life or at death (the unification of gift and estate taxes) is $12,920,000.

15. D: The cost basis of securities given as a gift depends both (1) on whether the original cost exceeds the donation-date FMV and (2) on what the final selling price is. If the original cost is less than the donation-date FMV, then the original cost becomes the donee's basis. If the original cost exceeds the donation-date FMV, then we look to the final selling price. If the final selling price exceeds the original cost, then the original cost becomes the basis. If the final selling price is between the original cost and the donation-date FMV, then the sale price itself becomes the basis (such that no gain or loss is recognized). If the final selling price is less than the donation-date FMV, then the donation-date FMV becomes the basis. For example, a stock was purchased for $100 but valued at $80 when donated. If the donee later sells it for $110, his capital gain is $110 – $100 = $10. If the donee later sells it for $90, he has no capital gain or loss ($90 – $90). If the donee later sells it for $65, his capital loss is $80 – $65 = $15.

16. B: The Securities Act of 1933 requires that investors receive financial and other significant information and that securities be registered, but it does not guarantee the information is accurate. The act also prohibits deceit, misrepresentation, and fraud in the sale of securities.

17. D: The New York Stock Exchange, NASDAQ Stock Market, and Chicago Board Options Exchange are all self-regulatory organizations (SROs).

18. D: Annual income, investment experience, and net worth should all be taken into consideration when determining investment suitability.

19. B: A certificate of deposit would be the most appropriate investment for an investor with an objective of capital preservation. Preferred stock can lose value just like common stock, so it wouldn't be a good investment for someone who wants to retain the value of the security. Bonds would not be the best way to preserve an investment because the value of bonds, both municipal and corporate, are directly tied to interest rates, which can rise or fall depending on economic circumstances.

20. C: Growth and income is another name for the investment objective of total return. Someone with a goal of capital preservation is known as a conservative investor.

21. D: An investor who invests a total of $25,000 between stocks, bonds, and mutual funds is the best example of diversification.

22. B: The modern portfolio theory does not guarantee against long-term losses.

23. D: Encrypted email, password-protected laptops, and printing only the last four digits of Social Security numbers on documents are all examples of information security to protect customers' personal information.

24. D: A common stock would be the least suitable investment for an elderly investor who is risk averse. While municipal bonds, corporate bonds, and mutual funds can lose their value, they are statistically less volatile than common stock.

25. D: A retired individual with an investment objective of income would be the investor best suited to invest in US Treasury bonds. US Treasury bonds, or T-Bills, are best suited for older, conservative investors because they are most likely to both retain their value and generate income. T-Bills are backed by the full faith and credit of the US government.

26. B: In a joint tenant with rights of survivorship (JTWROS) account, when the first person dies 100% of the assets remain with the surviving co-account holder.

27. D: Any authorized persons on an estate account are personal representatives.

28. C: Member firms must maintain client account statements for six years.

29. A: Multiple deposits that are immediately wired out of the account to a foreign bank would raise suspicions as a possible money laundering activity. All other choices are considered normal transactions and, therefore, not suspicious activity that could be seen on money laundering.

30. C: Money laundering is the process that criminals use to hide or disguise the source of their illegal money by converting it into funds that appear legitimate. Layering is the step in the money laundering process in which the criminal executes a sequence of transactions with the same money to obscure its origin. Structuring, or smurfing, is the process of dividing a larger transaction into smaller transactions to avoid triggering a reporting or recordkeeping requirement. Blackmail is a crime in which one threatens to reveal damaging information about another unless a large sum of money is paid.

31. D: The practice of buying and selling stocks rapidly throughout the day in the hope that the stocks will continue climbing or falling in value for the seconds to minutes that they are owned, allowing for quick profits to be made, is called day trading.

32. C: A municipal bond is not a suitable investment in an IRA. Since the account is tax deferred, there is no advantage to owning an investment that is tax free. Investors are required to pay taxes on earnings from common stock, corporate bonds, and mutual fund shares, so it would be worthwhile to purchase these through a tax-advantaged account such as an IRA.

33. B: Purchasing power risk is the possibility that higher prices in the future will reduce the amount of goods or services that may be bought. Market risk is the potential for loss due to the performance of the financial market. Financial risk is a generic term describing a variety of risk types, including credit risk, liquidity risk, and operational risk. Interest rate risk is the risk of investments losing value due to changes in prevailing interest rates.

34. B: Treasury stock is the name for stocks that have been sold and then repurchased (and held) by the issuing firm. Issued stock includes all company shares that have been sold to the public. Outstanding stock includes only those issued shares that are still held by the public (i.e., have not been repurchased by the company). Restricted stock are shares that are typically issued to people

143

within the company, such as executives or board members, as part of their compensation package. The shares are restricted in that there are limitations placed on when and how they may be traded.

35. B: Common stock is an equity investment representing ownership in a corporation. Corporate bonds give investors ownership of future cash flows, meaning companies owe investors the principal of the bonds, as well as interest, at a designated point in the future. A warrant and a right both give an investor the right but not the obligation to conduct a particular transaction.

36. D: An investor who currently owns 100 shares of stock will have 200 shares after the split.

37. C: A wash sale is defined as selling a security to generate a loss and then immediately buying the security back. It does not qualify as a capital loss (or tax loss sale) to reduce an individual's taxes.

38. B: A warrant is an option issued by a given company to buy one or more shares of common stock in that company at a price initially above the market price. A right is an option to buy one or more shares of common stock in a given company when new shares are issued, at a price initially below the market price. An option with the right to buy is known as a call option, and an option with the right to sell is known as a put option. Calls and puts are contracts made between participants in the marketplace rather than issued by a company.

39. D: The market in which securities are traded after they have been issued is the secondary market. The primary market is the market in which securities are sold by the issuers to investors. The money market is where investors trade short-term debt securities such as loans, MBSs, and bonds. The third market involves trading exchange-listed stocks through an over-the-counter (OTC) market.

40. D: Investing internationally has all of the same risks as investing in any security, including market and event risk. It also has foreign currency risk.

41. A: The last date that ABC Corporation stock can be purchased to receive the dividend is December 1. The record date is Monday, December 5, so that makes the ex-dividend date Friday, December 2. Since investors must own shares of the stock before the ex-dividend date to receive a dividend, the last day to purchase ABC Corporation stock would be Thursday, December 1.

42. C: The cost basis of 100 shares of stock purchased at \$35/share with an \$85 commission is \$3,585:

$$100 \times 35 + 85 = 3,585$$

43. A: Assets represent the resources of a company. A liability is an obligation, financial or otherwise, that the company owes to a person or business entity. Equity represents the amount of stockholders' capital that has been invested in a firm. Cash flow is the amount of cash moving into and out of a company.

44. B: The balance sheet is a summary report of a company's assets and liabilities, along with stockholder equity. The income statement reports a company's revenue over a specified time period, along with the expenses the company incurred to generate that revenue. The cash flow statement provides a summary of a company's cash flow and other events that caused changes in their cash position. An annual report is a document describing operations and financial position that every company listed on the stock market must provide to its shareholders.

45. B: Municipal bonds backed by the full faith and credit, and taxing power, of the issuer are called general obligation bonds. A revenue bond is a type of municipal bond that is backed by the future income of a specific municipal project that generates revenue. Agency bonds are issued by either an agency of the US government (other than the Treasury) or a government-sponsored enterprise (GSE) and may not be fully guaranteed. Treasury notes are bonds issued by the US Treasury and are backed by the full faith and credit of the US government.

46. D: A normal, upward-sloping yield curve indicates that yields tend to increase with longer maturities. It also shows that the longer the time span until maturity, the greater potential for price volatility and risk for loss. It does not indicate that short-term rates are higher than long-term rates.

47. B: Duration is the measure of bond price volatility that captures both price and reinvestment risks, indicating how a bond will react to different interest rate environments. Yield refers to the return on investment from a security. Immunization is a strategy used to mitigate risk and minimize the negative impact of changing interest rates. Beta is a calculated quantity that describes the volatility of a security by comparing its performance to that of the rest of the market.

48. D: The return on assets (ROA) is 5.29%.

$$\frac{\$18,000 \text{ (net profit after taxes)}}{\$340,000 \text{ (total assets)}} = 0.0529 = 5.29\%$$

49. D: The return on equity (ROE) is 10.59%.

$$\frac{\$18,000 \text{ (net profit after taxes)}}{\$170,000 \text{ (stockholder equity)}} = 0.1059 = 10.59\%$$

50. B: Ethics is the standard of conduct or moral judgment. Conscience refers to a person's internal sense of right and wrong. Values are a set of moral principals that influence a person's actions. The golden rule involves treating others in the way that you would want to be treated.

51. C: A market order is an order to buy or sell at the best available price at the time the order is placed. A limit order is an order to buy at or below a specific price or to sell at or above a specific price. A stop is an order to buy or sell a stock when its market price reaches or drops below a specified price. A stop limit order is an order to buy or sell at a specific price or better once a given stop price has been hit.

52. B: An order to sell at a specific price which is below the current market price is called a stop order. Answers A and C are examples of a market order. Answer D is an example of a limit order.

53. D: The broker-dealer is responsible for ensuring that clients receive the correct breakpoint.

54. A: Stock trades ordinarily settle on a T+2 schedule, meaning that the settlement date is two business days following the trade date (T). Therefore, a stock trade executed on Wednesday, December 31, would settle on Monday, January 5, which is two business days later since January 1 is a trading holiday and weekends do not count as business days.

55. D: The maximum amount that may be contributed to a 529 plan in TY 2023 is $17,000.

56. D: The tax consequence to an individual who rolls over his 401(K) directly to a traditional IRA is nothing. A direct rollover from a 401(K) to a traditional IRA is not a taxable event.

145

57. C: An individual who withdraws a lump sum from a qualified plan can avoid income taxes and penalties if the entire amount is rolled over into a traditional IRA within 60 days.

58. B: An individual must take his first required minimum distribution (RMD) by April 15 in the year following the year that he or she turns 70.5

59. C: The income limit for single individuals to contribute to a Roth IRA in TY 2023 is $153,000.

60. D: The price at which you can buy a security with a call is the strike price. The purchase price is how much investors pay for a security. The market price of a security is the current price it is being traded for on a given marketplace or exchange. Offering price refers to the stock price that investment banks initially set during an IPO.

61. A: The maximum profit the writer of an uncovered call option may realize is the premium received in exchange for the contract. The maximum loss is limitless. Writers of an uncovered option receive income via premiums for writing and selling option contracts without actually owning the underlying security. Uncovered calls are considered the riskiest types of option because the value of the security may increase infinitely and the investor must buy it to meet the call, so the eventual market price will determine the magnitude of their loss.

62. B: A security must be transferable from one individual to another and exposes the owner to risk and loss. Variable annuities are securities because they are transferable and, due to their payments being varied and unpredictable, expose the owner to some financial risk and variability in returns. Fixed annuities are not securities in that they provide for fixed payments, a guarantee on the receipt of earnings and principal, and consequently, no risk to the owner. Individual retirement accounts (IRAs) are not considered securities in that they provide for regular and predictable distributions to the owners, and thus, no risk.

63. C: Equity is interchangeable with the term *stock*, provides ownership for the investor, has no maturity, and is sold in order to provide capital to the issuing corporation.

64. A: Stock that is authorized for sale and sold to investors is issued stock, regardless of whether it still remains with investors or has subsequently been repurchased by the corporation. Authorized stock is the largest number of shares that can be sold by the corporation. Treasury stock is the stock that has been sold to the public and then repurchased by the corporation. Outstanding stock is stock that has been sold to investors and still remains with investors, having not been repurchased by the issuing corporation.

65. D: A registered representative would be committing a violation by rushing a customer to make a purchase solely to meet the ex-dividend date, recommending a purchase simply to benefit from a pending dividend, or promoting a stock by highlighting the benefit of the pending dividend while neglecting to educate him or her as to the fundamentals or appropriateness this stock may have as an investment.

66. D:

$$3 \times \$6 = \$18 \text{ per share}$$

Cumulative preferred shareholders always have priority over common stock shareholders in terms of dividend payment. They must receive both the missed dividend amounts as well as the current year's before PIX can pay any dividend to its common shareholders.

67. A:

$$\text{current yield} = \frac{\text{annual income}}{\text{current market price}}$$

$$\text{current yield} = \frac{(1.25 \times 4)}{52} = 0.096 = 9.6\%$$

68. D: The Federal Reserve may alter the level of money in circulation, actively transact in US government securities in the open market, and publicly share its views on the economy and the direction it sees it taking.

69. A: If the Federal Reserve were to increase the discount rate, all other rates would go up, demand would decrease, and ultimately, the economy would be slowed.

70. A: Lagging indicators take effect after the new direction of economy takes effect, take hold for a period of time, and provide confirmation about that change. Coincident indicators are an immediate result of even slight changes in the economy. Leading indicators occur prior to the economic change and can be looked to in order to analyze the future state of the economy.

71. C: A cyclical company is sensitive to the current state of the overall economy and reflects whatever that may be during periods of both high and low performance. A company in a defensive industry is the least sensitive to the state of the overall economy. A company in a growth industry will see faster growth than whatever the current state of the overall economy is.

72. B: Market orders do NOT guarantee a maximum or minimum executed price and in fact do not guarantee any specific price at all. Market orders can either be for a buy or sell order and are guaranteed to be filled immediately upon being introduced to the market and at the best possible price available.

73. B: The investor's order will be to buy 250 PPG 62.15 GTC DNR. The buy order remains exactly the same due to the investor stipulating the order to be do not reduce (DNR), and accordingly, the order will not be reduced to reflect the distribution of dividends.

74. A: Once quotes are published over the NASDAQ workstation, they must be honored. They are considered to be firm quotes, and a dealer refusing to honor his or her firm quotes is committing a violation known as backing away.

75. A: Pass-throughs provide investors with interest and principal payment income relative to their initial investments in pools of mortgages. The payments flow through to them on a monthly basis as the individual mortgages in the pools are paid down. A Separate Trading of Registered Interest and Principal of Securities (STRIP) is an investment that provides the opportunity to purchase separately either the principal or interest payment cash flow stream of a Treasury security. Collateralized mortgage obligations (CMOs) are similar to pass-throughs except that they are separated into different maturity schedules, or tranches, each being paid in full one at a time. Treasury inflation protected securities (TIPS) are securities whose interest payments and principal amounts are influenced by the level and movement of inflation.

How to Overcome Test Anxiety

Just the thought of taking a test is enough to make most people a little nervous. A test is an important event that can have a long-term impact on your future, so it's important to take it seriously and it's natural to feel anxious about performing well. But just because anxiety is normal, that doesn't mean that it's helpful in test taking, or that you should simply accept it as part of your life. Anxiety can have a variety of effects. These effects can be mild, like making you feel slightly nervous, or severe, like blocking your ability to focus or remember even a simple detail.

If you experience test anxiety—whether severe or mild—it's important to know how to beat it. To discover this, first you need to understand what causes test anxiety.

Causes of Test Anxiety

While we often think of anxiety as an uncontrollable emotional state, it can actually be caused by simple, practical things. One of the most common causes of test anxiety is that a person does not feel adequately prepared for their test. This feeling can be the result of many different issues such as poor study habits or lack of organization, but the most common culprit is time management. Starting to study too late, failing to organize your study time to cover all of the material, or being distracted while you study will mean that you're not well prepared for the test. This may lead to cramming the night before, which will cause you to be physically and mentally exhausted for the test. Poor time management also contributes to feelings of stress, fear, and hopelessness as you realize you are not well prepared but don't know what to do about it.

Other times, test anxiety is not related to your preparation for the test but comes from unresolved fear. This may be a past failure on a test, or poor performance on tests in general. It may come from comparing yourself to others who seem to be performing better or from the stress of living up to expectations. Anxiety may be driven by fears of the future—how failure on this test would affect your educational and career goals. These fears are often completely irrational, but they can still negatively impact your test performance.

> **Review Video: <u>3 Reasons You Have Test Anxiety</u>**
> Visit mometrix.com/academy and enter code: 428468

148

Elements of Test Anxiety

As mentioned earlier, test anxiety is considered to be an emotional state, but it has physical and mental components as well. Sometimes you may not even realize that you are suffering from test anxiety until you notice the physical symptoms. These can include trembling hands, rapid heartbeat, sweating, nausea, and tense muscles. Extreme anxiety may lead to fainting or vomiting. Obviously, any of these symptoms can have a negative impact on testing. It is important to recognize them as soon as they begin to occur so that you can address the problem before it damages your performance.

> **Review Video: 3 Ways to Tell You Have Test Anxiety**
> Visit mometrix.com/academy and enter code: 927847

The mental components of test anxiety include trouble focusing and inability to remember learned information. During a test, your mind is on high alert, which can help you recall information and stay focused for an extended period of time. However, anxiety interferes with your mind's natural processes, causing you to blank out, even on the questions you know well. The strain of testing during anxiety makes it difficult to stay focused, especially on a test that may take several hours. Extreme anxiety can take a huge mental toll, making it difficult not only to recall test information but even to understand the test questions or pull your thoughts together.

> **Review Video: How Test Anxiety Affects Memory**
> Visit mometrix.com/academy and enter code: 609003

Effects of Test Anxiety

Test anxiety is like a disease—if left untreated, it will get progressively worse. Anxiety leads to poor performance, and this reinforces the feelings of fear and failure, which in turn lead to poor performances on subsequent tests. It can grow from a mild nervousness to a crippling condition. If allowed to progress, test anxiety can have a big impact on your schooling, and consequently on your future.

Test anxiety can spread to other parts of your life. Anxiety on tests can become anxiety in any stressful situation, and blanking on a test can turn into panicking in a job situation. But fortunately, you don't have to let anxiety rule your testing and determine your grades. There are a number of relatively simple steps you can take to move past anxiety and function normally on a test and in the rest of life.

> **Review Video: How Test Anxiety Impacts Your Grades**
> Visit mometrix.com/academy and enter code: 939819

Physical Steps for Beating Test Anxiety

While test anxiety is a serious problem, the good news is that it can be overcome. It doesn't have to control your ability to think and remember information. While it may take time, you can begin taking steps today to beat anxiety.

Just as your first hint that you may be struggling with anxiety comes from the physical symptoms, the first step to treating it is also physical. Rest is crucial for having a clear, strong mind. If you are tired, it is much easier to give in to anxiety. But if you establish good sleep habits, your body and mind will be ready to perform optimally, without the strain of exhaustion. Additionally, sleeping well helps you to retain information better, so you're more likely to recall the answers when you see the test questions.

Getting good sleep means more than going to bed on time. It's important to allow your brain time to relax. Take study breaks from time to time so it doesn't get overworked, and don't study right before bed. Take time to rest your mind before trying to rest your body, or you may find it difficult to fall asleep.

> **Review Video: <u>The Importance of Sleep for Your Brain</u>**
> Visit mometrix.com/academy and enter code: 319338

Along with sleep, other aspects of physical health are important in preparing for a test. Good nutrition is vital for good brain function. Sugary foods and drinks may give a burst of energy but this burst is followed by a crash, both physically and emotionally. Instead, fuel your body with protein and vitamin-rich foods.

Also, drink plenty of water. Dehydration can lead to headaches and exhaustion, especially if your brain is already under stress from the rigors of the test. Particularly if your test is a long one, drink water during the breaks. And if possible, take an energy-boosting snack to eat between sections.

> **Review Video: <u>How Diet Can Affect your Mood</u>**
> Visit mometrix.com/academy and enter code: 624317

Along with sleep and diet, a third important part of physical health is exercise. Maintaining a steady workout schedule is helpful, but even taking 5-minute study breaks to walk can help get your blood pumping faster and clear your head. Exercise also releases endorphins, which contribute to a positive feeling and can help combat test anxiety.

When you nurture your physical health, you are also contributing to your mental health. If your body is healthy, your mind is much more likely to be healthy as well. So take time to rest, nourish your body with healthy food and water, and get moving as much as possible. Taking these physical steps will make you stronger and more able to take the mental steps necessary to overcome test anxiety.

Mental Steps for Beating Test Anxiety

Working on the mental side of test anxiety can be more challenging, but as with the physical side, there are clear steps you can take to overcome it. As mentioned earlier, test anxiety often stems from lack of preparation, so the obvious solution is to prepare for the test. Effective studying may be the most important weapon you have for beating test anxiety, but you can and should employ several other mental tools to combat fear.

First, boost your confidence by reminding yourself of past success—tests or projects that you aced. If you're putting as much effort into preparing for this test as you did for those, there's no reason you should expect to fail here. Work hard to prepare; then trust your preparation.

Second, surround yourself with encouraging people. It can be helpful to find a study group, but be sure that the people you're around will encourage a positive attitude. If you spend time with others who are anxious or cynical, this will only contribute to your own anxiety. Look for others who are motivated to study hard from a desire to succeed, not from a fear of failure.

Third, reward yourself. A test is physically and mentally tiring, even without anxiety, and it can be helpful to have something to look forward to. Plan an activity following the test, regardless of the outcome, such as going to a movie or getting ice cream.

When you are taking the test, if you find yourself beginning to feel anxious, remind yourself that you know the material. Visualize successfully completing the test. Then take a few deep, relaxing breaths and return to it. Work through the questions carefully but with confidence, knowing that you are capable of succeeding.

Developing a healthy mental approach to test taking will also aid in other areas of life. Test anxiety affects more than just the actual test—it can be damaging to your mental health and even contribute to depression. It's important to beat test anxiety before it becomes a problem for more than testing.

> **Review Video: Test Anxiety and Depression**
> Visit mometrix.com/academy and enter code: 904704

151

Study Strategy

Being prepared for the test is necessary to combat anxiety, but what does being prepared look like? You may study for hours on end and still not feel prepared. What you need is a strategy for test prep. The next few pages outline our recommended steps to help you plan out and conquer the challenge of preparation.

STEP 1: SCOPE OUT THE TEST

Learn everything you can about the format (multiple choice, essay, etc.) and what will be on the test. Gather any study materials, course outlines, or sample exams that may be available. Not only will this help you to prepare, but knowing what to expect can help to alleviate test anxiety.

STEP 2: MAP OUT THE MATERIAL

Look through the textbook or study guide and make note of how many chapters or sections it has. Then divide these over the time you have. For example, if a book has 15 chapters and you have five days to study, you need to cover three chapters each day. Even better, if you have the time, leave an extra day at the end for overall review after you have gone through the material in depth.

If time is limited, you may need to prioritize the material. Look through it and make note of which sections you think you already have a good grasp on, and which need review. While you are studying, skim quickly through the familiar sections and take more time on the challenging parts. Write out your plan so you don't get lost as you go. Having a written plan also helps you feel more in control of the study, so anxiety is less likely to arise from feeling overwhelmed at the amount to cover.

STEP 3: GATHER YOUR TOOLS

Decide what study method works best for you. Do you prefer to highlight in the book as you study and then go back over the highlighted portions? Or do you type out notes of the important information? Or is it helpful to make flashcards that you can carry with you? Assemble the pens, index cards, highlighters, post-it notes, and any other materials you may need so you won't be distracted by getting up to find things while you study.

If you're having a hard time retaining the information or organizing your notes, experiment with different methods. For example, try color-coding by subject with colored pens, highlighters, or post-it notes. If you learn better by hearing, try recording yourself reading your notes so you can listen while in the car, working out, or simply sitting at your desk. Ask a friend to quiz you from your flashcards, or try teaching someone the material to solidify it in your mind.

STEP 4: CREATE YOUR ENVIRONMENT

It's important to avoid distractions while you study. This includes both the obvious distractions like visitors and the subtle distractions like an uncomfortable chair (or a too-comfortable couch that makes you want to fall asleep). Set up the best study environment possible: good lighting and a comfortable work area. If background music helps you focus, you may want to turn it on, but otherwise keep the room quiet. If you are using a computer to take notes, be sure you don't have any other windows open, especially applications like social media, games, or anything else that could distract you. Silence your phone and turn off notifications. Be sure to keep water close by so you stay hydrated while you study (but avoid unhealthy drinks and snacks).

Also, take into account the best time of day to study. Are you freshest first thing in the morning? Try to set aside some time then to work through the material. Is your mind clearer in the afternoon or evening? Schedule your study session then. Another method is to study at the same time of day that you will take the test, so that your brain gets used to working on the material at that time and will be ready to focus at test time.

STEP 5: STUDY!

Once you have done all the study preparation, it's time to settle into the actual studying. Sit down, take a few moments to settle your mind so you can focus, and begin to follow your study plan. Don't give in to distractions or let yourself procrastinate. This is your time to prepare so you'll be ready to fearlessly approach the test. Make the most of the time and stay focused.

Of course, you don't want to burn out. If you study too long you may find that you're not retaining the information very well. Take regular study breaks. For example, taking five minutes out of every hour to walk briskly, breathing deeply and swinging your arms, can help your mind stay fresh.

As you get to the end of each chapter or section, it's a good idea to do a quick review. Remind yourself of what you learned and work on any difficult parts. When you feel that you've mastered the material, move on to the next part. At the end of your study session, briefly skim through your notes again.

But while review is helpful, cramming last minute is NOT. If at all possible, work ahead so that you won't need to fit all your study into the last day. Cramming overloads your brain with more information than it can process and retain, and your tired mind may struggle to recall even previously learned information when it is overwhelmed with last-minute study. Also, the urgent nature of cramming and the stress placed on your brain contribute to anxiety. You'll be more likely to go to the test feeling unprepared and having trouble thinking clearly.

So don't cram, and don't stay up late before the test, even just to review your notes at a leisurely pace. Your brain needs rest more than it needs to go over the information again. In fact, plan to finish your studies by noon or early afternoon the day before the test. Give your brain the rest of the day to relax or focus on other things, and get a good night's sleep. Then you will be fresh for the test and better able to recall what you've studied.

STEP 6: TAKE A PRACTICE TEST

Many courses offer sample tests, either online or in the study materials. This is an excellent resource to check whether you have mastered the material, as well as to prepare for the test format and environment.

Check the test format ahead of time: the number of questions, the type (multiple choice, free response, etc.), and the time limit. Then create a plan for working through them. For example, if you have 30 minutes to take a 60-question test, your limit is 30 seconds per question. Spend less time on the questions you know well so that you can take more time on the difficult ones.

If you have time to take several practice tests, take the first one open book, with no time limit. Work through the questions at your own pace and make sure you fully understand them. Gradually work up to taking a test under test conditions: sit at a desk with all study materials put away and set a timer. Pace yourself to make sure you finish the test with time to spare and go back to check your answers if you have time.

After each test, check your answers. On the questions you missed, be sure you understand why you missed them. Did you misread the question (tests can use tricky wording)? Did you forget the information? Or was it something you hadn't learned? Go back and study any shaky areas that the practice tests reveal.

Taking these tests not only helps with your grade, but also aids in combating test anxiety. If you're already used to the test conditions, you're less likely to worry about it, and working through tests until you're scoring well gives you a confidence boost. Go through the practice tests until you feel comfortable, and then you can go into the test knowing that you're ready for it.

Test Tips

On test day, you should be confident, knowing that you've prepared well and are ready to answer the questions. But aside from preparation, there are several test day strategies you can employ to maximize your performance.

First, as stated before, get a good night's sleep the night before the test (and for several nights before that, if possible). Go into the test with a fresh, alert mind rather than staying up late to study.

Try not to change too much about your normal routine on the day of the test. It's important to eat a nutritious breakfast, but if you normally don't eat breakfast at all, consider eating just a protein bar. If you're a coffee drinker, go ahead and have your normal coffee. Just make sure you time it so that the caffeine doesn't wear off right in the middle of your test. Avoid sugary beverages, and drink enough water to stay hydrated but not so much that you need a restroom break 10 minutes into the test. If your test isn't first thing in the morning, consider going for a walk or doing a light workout before the test to get your blood flowing.

Allow yourself enough time to get ready, and leave for the test with plenty of time to spare so you won't have the anxiety of scrambling to arrive in time. Another reason to be early is to select a good seat. It's helpful to sit away from doors and windows, which can be distracting. Find a good seat, get out your supplies, and settle your mind before the test begins.

When the test begins, start by going over the instructions carefully, even if you already know what to expect. Make sure you avoid any careless mistakes by following the directions.

Then begin working through the questions, pacing yourself as you've practiced. If you're not sure on an answer, don't spend too much time on it, and don't let it shake your confidence. Either skip it and come back later, or eliminate as many wrong answers as possible and guess among the remaining ones. Don't dwell on these questions as you continue—put them out of your mind and focus on what lies ahead.

Be sure to read all of the answer choices, even if you're sure the first one is the right answer. Sometimes you'll find a better one if you keep reading. But don't second-guess yourself if you do immediately know the answer. Your gut instinct is usually right. Don't let test anxiety rob you of the information you know.

If you have time at the end of the test (and if the test format allows), go back and review your answers. Be cautious about changing any, since your first instinct tends to be correct, but make sure you didn't misread any of the questions or accidentally mark the wrong answer choice. Look over any you skipped and make an educated guess.

At the end, leave the test feeling confident. You've done your best, so don't waste time worrying about your performance or wishing you could change anything. Instead, celebrate the successful

completion of this test. And finally, use this test to learn how to deal with anxiety even better next time.

> **Review Video: 5 Tips to Beat Test Anxiety**
> Visit mometrix.com/academy and enter code: 570656

Important Qualification

Not all anxiety is created equal. If your test anxiety is causing major issues in your life beyond the classroom or testing center, or if you are experiencing troubling physical symptoms related to your anxiety, it may be a sign of a serious physiological or psychological condition. If this sounds like your situation, we strongly encourage you to seek professional help.

Tell Us Your Story

We at Mometrix would like to extend our heartfelt thanks to you for letting us be a part of your journey. It is an honor to serve people from all walks of life, people like you, who are committed to building the best future they can for themselves.

We know that each person's situation is unique. But we also know that, whether you are a young student or a mother of four, you care about working to make your own life and the lives of those around you better.

That's why we want to hear your story.

We want to know why you're taking this test. We want to know about the trials you've gone through to get here. And we want to know about the successes you've experienced after taking and passing your test.

In addition to your story, which can be an inspiration both to us and to others, we value your feedback. We want to know both what you loved about our book and what you think we can improve on.

The team at Mometrix would be absolutely thrilled to hear from you! So please, send us an email at tellusyourstory@mometrix.com or visit us at mometrix.com/tellusyourstory.php and let's stay in touch.

Additional Bonus Material

Due to our efforts to try to keep this book to a manageable length, we've created a link that will give you access to all of your additional bonus material:

mometrix.com/bonus948/seriessie

157

Made in the USA
Monee, IL
13 August 2023

40947971R00092